Home Seller's Blues
And How To Beat Them

Home Seller's Blues
And How To Beat Them

JOAN GALE FRANK

Big Mouth Communications, LLC
Lake Oswego, Oregon

Big Mouth Communications, LLC
333 S. State Street, V-125, Lake Oswego, OR 97034
joanf@homesellersblues.com
www.homesellersblues.com

Disclaimer: This book is the outcome of years of research and home selling experience gathered by many people. I have done my very best to fill this book with relevant, usable information that can make the home selling experience, from start to finish, much easier. Although I think this information may make it easier and potentially faster to sell your home, I can't guarantee it will result in the sale of your property.

During the course of this book I also provide my understanding of certain real estate, financial, psychological, and other matters, but I'm not a professional in these areas and my information may not be applicable or appropriate to your particular circumstances. This book is not intended to provide you with personal advice, instead I urge you to seek qualified, expert advice in any area where you have concerns and questions relating to your situation. Your reliance on any of my statements and opinions is solely at your own risk. Big Mouth Communications and Joan Gale Frank are not liable for personal or financial loss or injury as a result of the information contained in this book.

Home Seller's Blues And How To Beat Them is a snapshot of what was available and going on during the time when it was written. The world is changing with lightning speed, so advice that may have made perfect sense when this book was created, may not make sense in the world you live in when you read this. (So those of you reading this in the year 2420, or maybe before, might find the business of real estate has changed somewhat.)

Finally, throughout this book I mention resources where you can find items that may be useful to you. However, with websites and businesses changing all the time, I can't guarantee that my references will be current when you go looking for them. If you use the services and resources listed, and by chance do not find them satisfactory, I take no responsibility for their products or services. But please do let me know about them, for I may remove these references from future book updates.

Here's What People Are Saying About *Home Seller's Blues*:

"We had our house on the market for 18 months before I discovered *Home Seller's Blues*. I sure wish I had access to this information sooner. It's made a big difference in my home selling attitude and also the entire feel of our house. And thanks for the door knob trick, I would never have thought of that!"
—*Sharon Hooper, Realtor*

"If you really want to sell your house for the best price in the shortest amount of time with the least amount of stress, you need to read this book. I have been a very successful 'listing agent' for the past 20 years in California and I would suggest Ms. Frank's book be given to every seller at the time of the listing appointment. Not only is this book important, it is entertaining and engaging to read."
—*Michele Affronte, Realtor*

"What a lifesaver this book has been! I felt better from page one. I was able to establish an action plan that not only helped me sell my house, but helped me continue to enjoy my life throughout the sales process. Thank you!"
—*Mary Kushner, Human Resource Manager and Home Seller*

"*Home Seller's Blues* is a must-read for anyone who is planning to sell or is in the midst of selling their home. Ms. Frank's insights into the emotions, psychology and real estate strategies of home selling are right on! She delivers with joy and humor, helping us to recognize that what we are feeling is universal. A must-read for anyone who is ready to move on with their lives and get their home sold."
—*Alexis Halmy, Principal Real Estate Broker*

"My wife bought this book and I didn't expect I'd actually read it. But then she couldn't take it away from me. I actually found myself laughing out loud while simultaneously picking up on tip after tip on how to make my house stand out from all the others for sale, without breaking the bank on home improvements. It also provided excellent, new ideas on how to promote my house to house hunters."

—*Harry Sarvasy, Electrical Engineer and Home Seller*

"I thought I had considered every aspect of home selling until I read this book. This is a fun and easy to read guide through all aspects of selling a home in today's topsy-turvy real estate market. The reader gets practical advice, self-help, coaching, and tough love to confront the hard to face issues of successfully selling a home. All bases are covered, from maximizing your views, to evaluating your real estate agent and practicing emotional self-care. She even provided a helpful checklist of what to do before every showing."

—*Leigh Merriman, Social Worker and Home Seller*

"If you're trying to sell your house, or even just thinking about it, you need a copy of *Home Seller's Blues*. In it, Joan Gale Frank has wisely and playfully detailed the pain, stress and worry that can come from having your house on the market for weeks, months or (heaven forbid) years. And she has a whole slew of strategies to both cope with and help move the process along. Her book is fun, easy to read and full of the kind of humor that keeps us breathing during stressful times. I found myself joyfully laughing out loud."

—*Shaeri Richards, Investment Property Owner*

Dedication

To my mother for a lifetime of astonishingly good advice, to my stepfather for his endless supply of wild and innovative ideas, and to my husband for his daily offerings of encouragement, laughter, computer intelligentsia, and extreme cuteness.

CONTENTS

Chapter Six   **120**

Chapter Seven   **143**

Chapter Eight   **153**

Chapter Nine   **161**

INTRODUCTION

My hope is that this book serves as a ray of hope, good cheer and practical advice if you're trying to sell your property but are having a tough time doing it. For whatever reason you're having trouble, whether it's because of a slow economy, an overstocked housing market or for other reasons particular to your property or area, my goal is to make the selling process easier to endure, and to make your home stand out in a buyer's mind so it sells faster.

I wrote this book because I was stuck with a house I couldn't sell for about a year and during that time I started manifesting a variety of discomforting symptoms: fretting, moaning, pacing, complaining, eating too many cookies, staging mini tantrums and feeling out of control of my life. Being that I'm not a big fan of suffering, I decided to make a project out of finding ways to ease these symptoms.

Unfortunately, when I went out looking for a book on this topic I couldn't find any. So I nominated myself to write one and then I seconded the motion. I felt I was a pretty good candidate to write this book for several reasons: first, as a marketing writer and consultant for the last 20 years, I had a lot of experience figuring out ways to make products irresistible. If I could make low-carb diet food and integrated circuits tempting, why not help people find new ways to sell their homes?

Second, I have a passion for pumping smart people for useful information, so I figured I could use this skill to find answers to many of my own home selling problems. And third, I've always found fast, inexpensive ways to beautify properties, because I'm allergic to spending big money on remodeling projects. As a result, I've come up with a bag full of tricks for how to make your property look great without emptying your wallet.

There's one more reason I wrote this book: as the author of the motivational program *Instant Guts!: How to Take a Risk and Win in Every Area of Your Life* I firmly believe it's important to take intelligent, strategic risks to get what you want out of life. Whether you're opening a new business, looking for a mate, or selling your house, the ability to take smart little risks can make all the difference in your outcome. As a result of this philosophy, you'll find this book is peppered with novel ideas that may not only help you sell your home faster, but also make your life a lot more fun while you're waiting.

Now, not every idea in this book is going to fit every reader, but I'd imagine that most everyone will find one or two, or 40 useful ideas for alleviating the Home Seller's Blues while increasing the attractiveness of your property and bringing new buyers to your front door.

Even if you don't have fifteen cents to spend on home improvement, that's okay. There's a lot you can do with what you already own, combined with a little creativity. But I do want to give you a wide range of ideas, from finding short-cuts that eliminate clutter (absolutely free) to installing hidden speakers in your garden to make it a musical paradise (this will cost you a little). Every reader gets to pick and choose how far they want to go.

And there's one more thing: my husband Jon would also like you to know that he was an integral part of the selling and home improvement process, but at times you might not know it because I use the "I" word instead of "we." I did this mainly because it sounds funny to say "we we we" all the time. So as you read on, please realize that my dear husband is lurking behind every page of this book. He played a big part in everything I talk about and he had to deal with the Home Seller's Blues just as much as I did.

Also, please do not ingest this book because it may contain nuts. Well, actually not a lot of nuts, but a bit of nutty flavor imparted by the author's writing style. However, the ideas in this book are tried and true, and have successfully brought comfort to many home sellers. You are in good hands.

I sincerely wish you the best in selling your property quickly and painlessly. Let's get going!

CHAPTER ONE

Behind Every "For Sale" Sign

Whether you're trying to sell a suburban tract house, a penthouse, or a trailer with an outhouse, being a home seller is a pain. You've got to clean and organize your home from top to bottom before you put it on the market. Then you've got to keep it clean, just in case a potential buyer comes by.

If you have a real estate agent, you've got to vacate your home on short notice (and bring the kids and dog with you) so your house can be shown without you in it. And you never know whether the next person who shows up on your doorstep is going to be the "One." You also have no idea how long it's going to take to sell your place, what kind of offer you'll get, or how long you'll be stuck in your current circumstances.

Then there's the frustration of getting excitedly optimistic before a showing, only to find out that the prospects never showed up. Or, some prospects tour your house three times, get your hopes up high, and then announce that they don't want to buy it because you don't have a big enough bathtub.

Meanwhile you are stuck paying your monthly mortgage, which may be increasing, along with property taxes, maintenance costs, and an ugly assortment of utility bills for a place you don't even want to be in anymore. You might also be watching your debt going up while your life savings are going down.

But wait, there's more! If property prices are falling in your area, you get to watch the erosion of your equity, knowing that vultures are circling, waiting for prices to drop even further before they swoop in and grab your house.

Then there's the added anxiety of watching other "For Sale" signs pop up overnight down the street from yours, signaling added competition. Especially if your neighbors price their houses lower, and have bigger bathtubs.

In a situation like this, you can start taking things personally. Even the most positive types can find themselves asking, "Why doesn't anyone want my house? Am I doing something wrong? Does my house have bad breath?"

On top of all of this, you've got to put your life on hold, stuck in limbo waiting, before you can move on and find new opportunities. All in all, it can add up to a pretty uncomfortable life experience . . . especially during a bad housing market, when your house can be on the market for months, or even years. It's a lot like dating. You don't know how long you'll have to wait for the right person to come along and it feels pretty much out of your control.

That was the experience my husband and I went through when we were trying to sell our house in Sedona, Arizona during a very slow market, in a wildfire-stricken area, in the middle of a three-year, city-wide road expansion project. All roads to our home were torn up and the stunning red rock views were obstructed by huge earth moving machines, deep open trenches and an obstacle course of grey concrete barriers and blinking detour signs. This did not help our home selling efforts.

Every day I'd cycle through a wide range of emotions. I'd wake up in the morning feeling somewhat optimistic and say, "I just know this house is going to sell." But by nightfall I'd grumble, "I think we're stuck here forever and they're going to have to bury us in the backyard." Then I'd spend the night sleepless and panicky—until the next morning when I'd find hope in the new day. It felt like I was becoming a schizophrenic lunatic.

I could imagine you saying to yourself as you read this, "Why didn't you take your house off the market?" "Couldn't you wait until things got better?" We couldn't. My husband and I had an extremely low adjustable mortgage rate that was about to adjust upward, along with a number of other expenses. We were also emotionally ready to move on because we owned a condo out of state and were looking forward to starting the next chapter in our lives there.

For all of these reasons, we decided to put the house on the market in the middle of this disastrous scenario. I couldn't help but wonder how all the other people going through this felt. Were they as upset as I was?

But it seemed other home sellers didn't want to talk about it. When I asked them they'd just say, "Yeah, it's a bit of a hassle" or "We've just got to wait it out." But no one confessed to midnight panic attacks and lunacy. And I never saw other home owners throwing temper tantrums next to their "For Sale" signs like I wanted to do—down on my knees, kicking and screaming and pounding my fists on the ground.

Instead I'd see my neighbors drive past their "For Sale" signs, and give me a little wave and a smile as they disappeared behind their remote controlled garage doors. It seemed they weren't bothered at all. Was it just me? Or did they break down once they got into the house, kicking and screaming behind closed doors?

Finally, someone told me the truth. A friend, who had had her house up for sale for 11 months before it finally sold, admitted that she cried every day her house was on the market. Eventually she began taking antidepressants because she was so miserable. When I asked her why she never mentioned it, she said she just didn't want to complain all of the time. Then, once the house was sold she wanted to forget the whole nasty episode and start a new life.

After much prodding, another friend confessed that her home selling experience depressed her from the moment the real estate agent pounded the "For Sale" sign into her front lawn. She felt it made her house feel unhappy and unloved, and it changed the entire feel of living there. The house no longer felt like her little sanctuary, but more like a piece of merchandise for sale. Until the house finally sold, she felt there was no place she could go to truly feel safe and at home.

Hearing these stories did make me feel better. Not because I enjoyed hearing tales of suffering, but because I discovered I wasn't alone in my thoughts after all. But for some reason most people didn't want to bring it up. However, once I was able to get people talking, quite a few admitted that they also felt they were the only ones going through it. Everyone else, they assumed, was able to handle it just fine.

Being I'd much rather feel happy than keep suffering, I decided there had to be relief from this situation. Whether I'm cleaning out the garage, doing my taxes, or going to the dentist, I always look for ways to make a situation more fun, or into a game, or at least find some humor in it. (For example, the way to make dental drilling more enjoyable is to bring a music player and headphones, crank up the volume, and tune into something that matches the sound of the drill, only with a better beat.) So why not find a way to make this rotten, anxiety-provoking, disgusting home selling experience more enjoyable? I decided to make this my mission.

You're Not in This Alone

My first stop was the local bookstore. In the real estate section there were rows of books on how to buy, sell, fix and flip properties, but there wasn't one book on how to handle *not* being able to sell your home. Then I went to the self-help section. I found loads of books on getting out of a rut and how to separate from your spouse, but not one book on how to separate from your house.

Then I looked online for help. I found local and national support groups for practically every possible physical or mental condition, along with the condition's official acronym. For example, if you grind your teeth and have trouble with your jaw, you suffer from TMJ (Temporomandibular Joint Disorder). If you have restless legs, you have RLS (Restless Leg Syndrome). If you can't stand dark winters, you've got Seasonal Affective Disorder (SAD). If you suffer from a general anxiety disorder, you'll be diagnosed with the creatively termed condition, "General Anxiety Disorder" or GAD. There's even a diagnosis called "NDA," which means "No Diagnosis of Anything."

But those of us who are stuck with a house that won't sell, who are feeling anxious, sleepless, depressed, out-of-control, financially stressed, and sick of constantly cleaning—we are on our own. There's no book, no support group, not even an acronym to confirm what we are going through.

So I decided it was high time to take the situation into our own hands, starting by acknowledging the condition and giving it a name we can all be proud of. My first thought was "People Trying To Sell Their Homes But Having A Rotten, Anxiety-Provoking, Disgusting Experience Syndrome." The acronym for this was "PTTSTHBHARAPDES" but some people said they had trouble remembering it, so I shortened it to Home Seller's Blues (HSB).

There you have it. For those of you who suspect you have HSB, welcome to our group. You are not alone. You are with millions of other good, honest, well-meaning people who understand what you are going through. Now don't you feel better?

It's similar to going to a doctor and discovering that your symptoms are not just in your head. They are part of a recognized condition that experts have identified. As a person with HSB, you're likely to be suffering from a full range of disturbing mental, emotional, physical and financial symptoms that can be alleviated. You are also fully entitled to educate others about the condition and use your newfound acronym both at home and at cocktail parties. You can now stand tall and announce "I have HSB."

Finally, I Discover Answers

Being that there were no ready-made answers on how to cope with HSB, I went out looking for expert advice. I talked with real estate agents, professional home stagers, landscapers, marketing consultants, psychologists, counselors, financial advisors, a gang of motivational coaches, successful home sellers who had sold their properties during real estate downturns, and a psychic from Sedona who channeled a disembodied entity from circa 600 B.C. None of these specialists had the complete answer, but together they each held a piece of the puzzle.

This book is the outcome of all of their knowledge and advice. Through their help, I was able to beat my own case of HSB and sell my house in the dead of winter, during a time when there was a glut of other houses on the market.

What made it even better was that our home sale was a win-win for everyone. The new buyers were thrilled to find a unique, irresistible home that was perfect for their needs. And, I can't tell you how great it felt to be free to move on with my life. Free from scary, mounting bills, free from looking out at that "For Sale" sign!

After we sold our house, other desperate home sellers in the area asked, "How did you do that?" It seemed a shame to keep all of this information to myself, especially if I could show them how to sell their home faster than, say, the house down the street with the bigger bathtub. So I decided to tell all.

Here is everything I learned and what you'll get from reading this book:

- How to stay in control of your life—instead of feeling stuck in limbo while your house is on the market.
- How to attract the greatest number of interested buyers to your front door.
- How to make your house look beautiful and unique while spending the least amount of money and time.
- How to get people to fall in love with your house, even if there is a glut of other homes on the market in your area.
- How to get your home ready to show in ten minutes or less.
- How to get the highest offer price possible—as quickly as possible.

- When to lower your house price and why, and when not to.
- How to reduce financial fears while your house is on the market.
- How to reduce anxiety and midnight panic attacks.
- How to live more comfortably with uncertainty.
- How to actually have fun and make the home selling experience a productive, happy time in your life.

Who This Book Will Help:

- **Those without "For Sale" signs on their property yet**

  If you're considering putting your property on the market and want to make your home as irresistible as possible, while avoiding the Home Seller's Blues (HSB), this book is for you.

- **Those with "For Sale" signs currently on display**

  If you currently have your property on the market and would like immediate solutions for beating HSB and selling your property faster, this book is for you.

- **Those who had a "For Sale" sign, but gave up and took it down**

  If you tried selling your house and couldn't, but are considering whether to put it back on the market again or stay where you are, this book will give you creative ideas and newfound hope, no matter which option you choose.

- **Third parties who are assisting others in home sales**

  If you are a real estate agent, broker, or you're involved in any other way with selling a house that isn't yours, this information can make it faster and easier to close a deal. It will also help you understand the seller's HSB symptoms so that you can offer them comforting advice.

- **Those who aren't selling now, but want to beautify their homes inexpensively**

Even if your home isn't on the market and you don't plan on selling soon, this book is packed with quick, easy ways to make your home a joy to live in every single day. And, if or when you do decide to sell, you'll have an attractive, marketable home ready to go, without having to invest extra time, money or effort getting it ready.

No matter which category you fit into, this book can help you decide what to do next. But before we go any further, it's time to measure your own HSB level.

Symptoms of Home Seller's Blues

Just how bad is your HSB? Take a look at each of the Home Seller's Blues symptoms below and give yourself a point for each statement that you agree with. Then add up your points to determine your HSB level, as described after the quiz.

The Home Seller's Blues Quiz

1. _____ You find yourself frequently wiping down your countertops and sinks, just in case someone comes by to see your property.

2. _____ At times you stop cleaning and let the dirt just stay where it is. You think, "Why bother cleaning again? No one is ever going to come by anyway!"

3. _____ When leaving your home, you hide your valuables and unattractive items in case there is a showing. But then you forget where you've hidden them. As a result, you can't find your credit card bill, bank statement or ripe bananas, until it's too late.

---

4. _____ At times you don't want to even leave your house because you're so tired of cleaning before you go out for the day. Instead you stay home depressed and in a mess.

5. _____ You get a little nervous when you boil eggs, fry fish, or steam cauliflower because you don't want a potential buyer to come by and think your house (or someone in it) stinks.

6. _____ You get a little nervous when the phone rings. If it's a real estate agent it means you have to stop what you're doing and get ready for a showing. If it's a friend you are slightly disappointed because it isn't an agent. If it's an agent with an offer, this can spell the beginning of nerve-racking negotiations, exhausting packing and the trauma of moving.

7. _____ You feel forlorn when your spouse calls to tell you, "Good news! We've just won a trip to Paris" when you'd much rather hear, "Good news! We've just got an offer on the house!"

8. _____ You find it difficult to make plans or arrange for a vacation in advance, just in case you might be in the middle of moving.

9. _____ You're afraid to walk out of the shower naked just in case you didn't hear the doorbell or phone announcing that a real estate agent was coming through your house with a client.

10. _____ You discover the house down the street, which went on the market long after yours, just sold. And to make it worse, you get to watch your neighbor's moving truck come and go, while you stand next to your fading "For Sale" sign, waving goodbye.

Scoring Your HSB Symptoms

0 points: You either do not have your property on the market, or it has been on the market for less than 15 minutes.

1 to 3 points: You have a touch of HSB. Your house has probably been on the market for two months or less, or you have been happily distracted by something else, such as a new relationship, a Ferrari, or Botox®. The trick for you is to keep focusing on the good stuff while simultaneously figuring out how to make your property stand out to potential buyers. The quicker you sell your property, the less chance your HSB score will rise.

4 to 7 points: Uh-oh. Your HSB level concerns me. You may feel like you've had your house on the market for decades, even if you've only been trying to sell it for three to six months. You need to add some fun diversions to your life to get your mind off your HSB symptoms. Instead of dwelling on the uncertainty of when your property is going to sell, focus on enjoyable, controllable things you can do right now: enroll in a community college course or night class to learn something new, read distracting novels, or make something big and chocolate with at least seven layers. Be sure to pay close attention to chapter two, where I discuss pricing your home. It might be that a little price reduction, although seemingly painful, could result in a quicker sale and exciting new beginnings for you.

Over 8 points: Poor baby. You have a full-blown case of HSB, which can grow even worse if you don't proactively make changes in your life. It's important to be creative and think outside the box in terms of possible new financial and living options. Remember that during challenging times like these, you're often able to grow in surprising new ways. Translate this time of crisis into a time of creative opportunities. Like a hero in your own story with your back up against the wall, you can prevail! Also, be sure to take good care of yourself. Get exercise, eat right, and talk with others about your situation. And for best results, don't just read this book, DO what it says!

Now that you know whether you have HSB or not, there is one more thing that might make you feel a bit better: having HSB is completely natural and biological because people don't like to be stuck. It's built right into the core of our being. In this next section, you'll find out why.

No Wonder Home Sellers Get Crabby

It's an unnatural state for any living thing to not be able to move when the desire strikes. Most animals are free to roam the plains, cross the mountains, swim the oceans and navigate the skies. There are even trees in the Amazon, known as "walking trees" that grow new appendages, enabling them to slowly relocate themselves to areas where they'll get more sunlight.

Or, consider the ever-practical hermit crab. If this crab wants to move to a different shell, all it has to do is find a new one it likes better, pull up next to it, crawl out of the old shell and scoot into the new one. Moving day is over, and the crab goes on with its interesting life. The crab doesn't have to wait for another crab to pre-qualify for a loan, or pull the equity from its current shell to get the necessary down payment to upsize to a bigger shell. (Or, perhaps downsize to a smaller one.)

For most of history, people have also been able to move whenever they've wanted. If their resources ran low, the water supply dried up, or too many strangers crowded into their territory, all they had to do was pack up their belongings and move on to better opportunities elsewhere. That's why humans have migrated to practically every corner of the globe.

But now, for the vast majority of people, we've become imprisoned by our property. If our equity is tied up in our homes, most of us don't want to walk away and lose it, no matter how much we desire to move on. No wonder home sellers feel anxious and blue! It's against the natural order of life to be stuck in a house!

But—there is good news: we have much more control over our life circumstances than a crab does. A crab doesn't know anything about home décor, pricing or niche marketing. (Especially soft shell crabs, they're the worst.)

How We Differ From Crabs:

Yes, being stuck with a property isn't fun, but you really do have a lot more control than you may think. This book will help you realize that you have a great many choices in the matter. Just knowing you have choices can shift your entire attitude, and as a result, it can help change your circumstances.

Ten Big Things You Have Control Over:

1. You have control over the asking and selling price of your home.

2. You have control over the appearance and condition of your home.

3. You have control over the sales representation of your home. (Yourself or an outside agent.)

4. You have control over the marketing and advertising of your home.
5. You have control over the terms of sale of your home.
6. You have control over your attitudes and perspective of the situation.
7. You have control over how you're going to live your life during the home selling process.
8. You have control over creating new solutions to solve your financial problems.
9. You have control over whether to keep your house on the market or take it off for a month, a year, or longer if appropriate.
10. You have control over your decision to make the home selling experience an awful time or an innovative, productive, enjoyable time.

We will be discussing each of these forms of control in this book. In the next chapter we'll start with the most difficult, gruesome issue: pricing your home.

CHAPTER TWO

What to Write on Your Price Tag

Pricing your home can be a very challenging issue. It can make grown women cry and bristly-bearded men whimper, because it all boils down to one question . . . Are you willing or able to reduce your price to the point where you have the best possible chance of selling your home quickly?

Why Would I Want to Sell My Home For Less?

The decision you make on your home price may make the difference between packing your belongings and moving out within weeks, or sitting on it for months, or even years. Obviously, no one likes lowering one's price. Who wants to make less money? But there may be so much more to your financial and life equation than just the monetary price you want to get right now.

Home sellers can be categorized into two groups:

Group One: Those who have had their property price appreciate since they bought their homes and therefore expect to reap a profit. (That is, if they haven't taken out too many equity loans that have eaten up their profit.)

Group Two: Those who have seen their home prices depreciate since they purchased. (And may have also taken out equity loans that have used up any previously expected profit.)

If you're in the first group, you clearly have more wiggle room to adjust the price of your property, and you might still be able to realize a profit. So the big question for you is, can you handle making less money, and possibly readjust your financial plans as a trade-off for getting on with the rest of your life sooner?

If you're in the second group, it's understandable why you don't want to offer your property at a lower price. Every dollar you take off is a dollar you'll most likely have to pay back when you sell, especially if you factor in closing costs, commissions and other expenses. If you can come up with ways to pay your ongoing bills, and you think the housing market is bound to improve, you might want to hold off selling your house. That way you won't lose your shirt by selling too low.

However, if you're falling further and further behind financially, and are concerned that prices may slip even further, it might make sense to sell your property now at a price that will get it sold sooner than later. What you don't want is to keep your price high, get further into debt, then a year from now discover that your house is worth even less, your debt is worth more, and you're in danger of a foreclosure. (Now that's ugly.)

In other words, whether you have made a profit on your home or not, you should consider lowering your property price if you're concerned that prices are on a long-term downhill slide, and if you wait, you'll just get less or possibly lose what you have.

The biggest mistake sellers make is to lower their property

price too little, too late. This is a really important statement, so I will repeat it for emphasis:

The biggest mistake sellers make is to lower their property price too little, too late.

Many people feel that they'll start with a higher price, but accept a lower price if someone makes them an offer. The problem is many prospects won't even consider looking at your house if it's priced too high—especially in a buyer's market where people are expecting good deals. Then, all you've done by keeping your property price high is to eliminate a segment of the market who might have come to see it. Most buyers like to take the path of least resistance. Why go after a house that costs more, and hope to negotiate a better deal when there are already lots of houses available at lower prices?

In addition, buyers look at homes within certain price ranges, for example, $249,000 to $299,000. If you price your property at $310,000, but are ready to accept an offer for $295,000, then you've just eliminated a number of people who won't look at houses priced over $300,000.

Whether you stand to make a profit or not, there are a number of other reasons why you should consider lowering the asking price of your property. Many of these go beyond monetary reasons.

Nine Good Reasons to Lower Your Asking Price (Sooner Rather than Later)

- **Your house stands out in comparison to others**

When there are a lot of houses on the market, buyers have a tremendous number of places they can view. Many real estate agents say that the average number of homes they typically show a buyer in one day is about six. After that, most people's brains get overloaded and the properties begin blending together into a mush. That's when buyers start asking questions such as, "Was it the fifth or sixth house that had that awful kitchen?"

Agents also report that the average number of properties a serious buyer sees before making an offer is between 12 and 20. After that, buyers think they have a pretty good idea of what they can get for their money and they start getting bored of the hunting process. After they've seen 20 properties, they assume the next 20 won't be that much different.

What this means is, unless you're in the top 20, the chance of your house being shown diminishes. And in a tough housing market, when people are looking for bargains, they are most likely to view the 20 properties that are the best deals. Unless your house makes it into that group, you take the chance of not having your house shown very often.

Real estate agents also keep their eyes open for good property buys because it gives them a better chance of making a sale. And when agents are hungry, you can bet they are going to show the properties that are the best buys available. Especially if an agent can enthusiastically tell their clients that a place is "priced below appraisal" or is "the lowest price per square foot in the area."

A lower property price makes you stand out in print and online advertising as well. Use an attention-grabbing phrase such as "priced below appraisal" and prospects will circle, highlight or print out your property information and pay you a visit.

You also want to make sure that you don't "follow the market down." In other words, you don't want to drop your price at the same time, and for the same amount that other owners are dropping their prices. That just keeps you in the middle of the pack. This is a terrible fate, because not only do you *not* stand out, even though you've lowered your price repeatedly, your house stays on the market longer and longer and is worth less and less. It is much better to do a preemptive strike and lower your asking price *before* others do. That way you'll have the best chance of getting your house shown and sold.

■ Because life is precious and time is priceless

How much are the days, months and years of your life worth? If you're sitting around waiting for your house to sell then you may be wasting the most valuable possession you own: your time. People can find ways to re-make money they've lost, but there's no way to recapture lost time. You will never get those lost months or years of your life back again, no matter how clever you are.

Plus, the time that you spend waiting for your house to sell could be better used to advance your life in new ways. Also, ask yourself which situation would create better memories: Months lived in limbo, waiting for your house to sell? Or, months spent exploring new places, pursuing exciting opportunities, and making new friends as a result of selling for a little less and moving on with your life?

■ You can reduce (or eliminate) your financial stress

Everyone knows that stress isn't good for your body. It can keep you up at night and then ruin your day, lowering your energy level and negatively coloring much of what you do and think. Who needs that?

One woman I interviewed said she was under so much

pressure before she sold her home that her body fell apart. She had heart palpitations and neck and back pain because her shoulders were permanently riding up around her ears. After more than a year of waiting for her house to sell, she had accumulated $36,000 in debt on top of her rising monthly bills.

Finally she decided to lower her asking price a little below the other houses in her area. It worked! After the home was sold she paid off all of her debts and rented a small house. No more big bills in the mailbox. No more midnight worries. She was amazed at how light and free she suddenly felt. She actually found herself skipping from room to room with a big smile on her face. All because she was willing to slash the price on her property and move on.

■ You can have peace of mind in a world full of troubles

If you worry about negative trends, such as domestic and global economic problems, the oil crisis, terrorist attacks, or increased destructive weather patterns, you may not want to be stuck in a house that keeps you from moving away and readjusting your life and finances. This is especially true if your primary nest egg is tied up in your property.

If you're concerned about what the future holds, selling your property for a little less now may help you avoid selling it for even less later when fewer interested buyers may be around. If these negative thoughts worry you, getting out from under your house may give you peace of mind. You can then decide where and how you want to live and change your life accordingly, instead of waiting until the "bottom drops out."

I'm not saying this is going to happen of course, and no one has a crystal ball to foretell the future, but with the gloom and doom reports you hear on the news, it's understandable that many people can feel this way.

■ You can stop living in limbo and uncertainty

When you don't know when you're going to move, you might put off doing things, such as joining a club, taking classes or doing anything else that involves making a long-term commitment. You're also less likely to join a gym or golf course that requires paying an initiation fee, which would be wasted if you moved out of the area.

In addition, you might not want to make new friends if you think you're just going to leave them in several months anyway. And, if you want to start or enlarge an existing business, you might hold off because you'll just have to re-establish yourself all over again in your new location. Why make business cards if you plan to change your address and phone number soon?

As a result of holding off, your life begins to stagnate. It's easy to become less social and lose your momentum and drive, which just makes you feel more out of control. You might even forget what your dreams and goals are altogether. Over time, your personality can actually change. It doesn't happen over-night, but as the months go by, it can have a big impact. You can go from being a happy social butterfly to a depressed shut-in while your "For Sale" sign swings in the breeze.

By reducing your sales price and potentially selling faster, you can cut down on all of this uncertainty. Instead of using up your energy worrying, you can redirect it into your new life.

- **You can stop worrying about keeping your house ready to show**

As nice as it is to have a clean house, let's face it, it can be a drag to constantly have to clean every room of your house, sweep the leaves off your driveway and pull every weed out of your flowerbeds. And, every time you step out of your house for more than a few minutes you have to worry, "Did I hide my iPod and jewelry? Is the floor vacuumed?"

It eats up a lot of time and energy keeping up with these things. Then there's the frustration of doing big "emergency" house cleanings for showings that don't amount to anything. By selling your house at a lower price faster, you can skip months of this game and make your dust rags and sponges last much longer.

- **It's easier to negotiate an "as-is" offer**

When you give buyers a great price on your property, they may have less bargaining power over what you have to fix and repair before the deal closes. If a buyer pays a higher price, they often stand firm on what they want you to fix before they move in.

By pricing your house lower, you can put yourself in a stronger negotiating position. One woman I talked with told me she accepted an offer for $15,000 less than what she had asked for. When the inspections came back, revealing a list of items that should be fixed, she reminded the buyers that she had already given them quite a bit off the price. The buyers acknowledged this and agreed to do the repairs on their own.

This ended up saving the seller a lot of time and out-of-pocket expenses. Plus, it freed her up to pack and start looking for her next place, instead of spending her time fixing the home she was leaving.

- ■ **You can make up the price difference on another property**

There is good news when times are tough in the real estate market. You're not the only one who has to lower your home price. Other sellers with properties that you might want to buy have to lower their prices too. This means you can get a good deal on your next property and you might be able to make up the difference in what you lost when you sold your home for less.

Let's say you sold your house for $50,000 less than what you wanted, so you moan and groan while you're packing up. But then you go out looking for a new place and find one that has also been reduced by $50,000. In a sense, you've just broken even. And, if the seller takes an even lower offer, you might come out ahead of the game.

If by chance you're moving up to a more expensive home, a price drop of 20%, for example, on the bigger home could equate to quite a big savings. If the home (for fantasy sake) was originally priced at $1 million, but is now priced at $800,000, you've saved $200,000 on that house. Later, when or if the housing market picks back up, you can realize a large appreciation without having to do any home improvement projects.

So the moral of the story is that sometimes you need to take a step back in order to move two steps forward. Besides, wouldn't you rather be a buyer in a bad market than a stuck seller?

- **You can avoid a short sale or foreclosure scenario**

If you price your home at an attractive, competitive price from the start, instead of lowering it later if prices continue to fall, you may sell your home sooner and avoid the possibility of losing everything. I've seen this happen firsthand, where one set of neighbors reduce their home price and sell, while the other neighbors hold out for a higher price.

The first set of neighbors move on with their life. The second set keep waiting while property values drop lower and their home ends up worth potentially less than their mortgage. If these second neighbors also face financial difficulties, such as an unexpected job loss or increased expenses, combined with an underwater mortgage, they can end up losing their property. If they had set a lower price to begin with, they may have been the ones who sold their home and moved on . . . instead of their "luckier" neighbors.

Choosing The Perfect Selling Price

The first thing you want to do when deciding on a price for your property is to take a look at the comps—the real estate report listing the prices of comparable properties in your area. If possible, get the comps for properties sold or listed on your street. Property prices can differ widely, even if you're just a few blocks away from the other properties. This is especially true if you live next to a dividing line that separates such things as school districts or housing developments.

By viewing the comps, you'll get a general idea of what properties similar to yours in size, location and age have sold for, or are currently selling for. If you're serious about selling as fast as possible, then you will want to be one of the lower priced offerings, or the lowest in your category of similar offerings.

Even in a slow housing market, a house that is attractively priced can sell quickly. After all, people have to live somewhere and many prefer owning a house to renting. They might choose your location because they have friends or family close by, work in the area, or would like to be adjacent to certain amenities in your location. So as you can see, even if you think there's no one out there interested in your home, you might be thrilled to discover your house is a perfect fit for someone—if it's priced right.

One way to make a low price stick out is to price your house so that it's either the lowest price per square foot, or priced below appraisal. This of course requires you to get your home professionally appraised so that you know how much it's worth and how much to knock off. The appraiser can give you an independent, non-biased opinion, taking into account such factors as the health of the real estate market in your area, local amenities such as whether it's in a good school district, and the general condition, size and features of your home.

Getting an accurate appraisal price *before* your property goes on the market can also keep a deal from falling through. If you and a prospective home buyer agree on an offer price that is higher that a loan provider's appraisal price—the buyer won't be able to get a loan and your deal can fall through. Then you'll be back at square one, suffering from an even worse case of the Home Seller's Blues.

Another valuable measurement for determining your asking price is to go house hunting yourself. Visit open houses and gather flyers from other homes in your neighborhood. If you have a real estate agent, ask him or her to take you to see comparable properties in your same price range. This way you can see with your own eyes how much an equal amount of money can buy. Also take a look at properties priced slightly above and below your range to get a feel for what a little more or less will buy.

If you find many similar properties priced around the same range as yours, it can mean it'll take longer to sell your place because other houses are competing for the same buyers as you are. And, if there aren't many people looking, it can take a long time until a buyer decides that of all the houses available, yours is the right one.

If you see houses for sale that are nicer than yours, but offered around the same price, you need to say "uh-oh" and do some quick thinking about lowering your numbers. Be very honest, you might see a property that you think isn't as nice as yours listed for more. But ask yourself, is it in a better location? Does it have more land or maybe a better view?

Also look at the number of days a property has been on the market. If a place has been sitting around for months, it can mean the sellers aren't that motivated to sell. They might not mind waiting until they eventually get the price they want.

But if you really want or need to get out, then your best bet is to lead the pack as the low price leader. Never mind what the others are doing—especially if you already stand to make a profit, even if you sell at a lower price.

By setting your price lower, yours can be the property that real estate agents will show their clients the first day they go out looking. In fact, it might even be an agent who buys your house.

$5,000 at-a-Time: Going, Going, Gone!

Some people may not be able stomach lowering the price a dramatic amount all at once, and if this is you, here is another approach that you might like better: reduce your price $5,000 a week, or for a low percentage of its cost, until someone grabs it. (For example, if your home is on the market for $199,000, a 1% price reduction equals about $2,000 off.) This serves several purposes:

First, you constantly keep your name in front of the real estate brokers and agents because they see your new price on their weekly hot sheets that highlight new properties plus those that have just lowered their prices. You can also include this information in your advertisements to the public.

Second, by lowering your price one step at a time, you can start at a higher price and incrementally go down, potentially enabling you to get a better offer than if you started out at your lowest price. This method is like a reverse auction where the auctioneer yells, "Do I hear $200,000 for this house? Okay, how about $195,000? No takers? Then how about $190,000? SOLD to the lady in green!"

The downside of trying this approach, however, is that if there are a lot of houses on the market already at competitive prices, it will take you a while to get down to their level. And, if the market experiences any further downturn, you'll end up having to keep following it down just to stay competitive. In this case, you may end up having to lower your price beyond what you would have, if you had just started at a lower price to begin with.

How the $5,000 (or Percentage) At-a-Time Strategy Works

Here is an actual case study of two couples living next door to each other, both trying to sell their houses in California. (Their names have been changed to protect their anonymity.) Let me introduce you:

First, meet Dick and Jane who own a 4,000 square foot, 30 year-old wreck-of-a-house. It has musty smelling lime green carpet, warped wooden cabinets, cracking linoleum, a splintering sagging deck and a baffling room layout.

Next, meet Anthony and Cleopatra who built a gorgeous showplace of a home two years ago, right next door to Dick and Jane's house. Anthony and Cleopatra's home is also 4,000 square feet, but their house has a dream gourmet kitchen with a granite island the size of Manhattan, high-end appliances, travertine tile floors, big modern bathrooms with giant Jacuzzi tubs, deep walk-in closets and extremely expensive window treatments. The "wow" factor of this house is off the scale.

Anthony and Cleopatra list their house for $875,000. They actually wanted to ask for $900,000, but because the market is a little slow, they decide to keep it in the $800,000 range. Their real estate agent agrees it's a good price for such a house.

Six months go by. The house with all its wondrous features doesn't receive one offer, even though many people come by and say, "oooh, ahhhh!" So Anthony and Cleopatra decide to take the brave step and lower their house to $849,000.

Still no takers. Cleopatra wants to tear her hair out. Anthony wants many beers.

At this point, their neighbors Dick and Jane put their old wreck-of-a-house on the market and list it for $800,000. Anthony and Cleopatra can't believe that Dick and Jane could possibly list their place for only $49,000 less than their beautiful home. "Our top-of-the-line appliances and granite countertops are worth that alone!" Cleopatra scoffs.

But that's when things start to get interesting: the following week, Dick and Jane reduce their price by $5,000, which puts it back on the Realtor Hot Sheet and back in the forefront of the agents' minds. As each week passes, Dick and Jane reduce their price another $5,000 and within three months they receive and accept an offer for $730,000.

Dick and Jane go out and celebrate. They have sold their old house in a slow market for a pretty good price.

Anthony and Cleopatra peep through their expensive window treatments as Dick and Jane's moving company empties the house. Then they watch as their neighbors drive off into the sunset to start their new live's elsewhere.

After several more months have passed, Anthony and Cleopatra's agent urges them to reduce their price to $795,000. They are both horrified. It would mean a price drop of $54,000 more, but they do it because their Home Seller's Blues symptoms are getting worse and they want OUT.

But still no offers come in. They also notice that other home owners in the area are lowering their prices at an accelerated rate so they start getting nervous.

One fateful day, Anthony and Cleopatra get an offer. It's an offer for $750,000—which is another $45,000 price drop. But they grab it anyway because prices are continuing to drop while the inventory of houses is climbing. Besides, their house has now been on the market for 11 months and they are tired of waiting.

When all is said and done, Anthony and Cleopatra end up selling their beautiful showplace of a home for only $20,000 more than their neighbor's ugly old wreck—and it took them eight months longer and a lot more heartache to do it.

Had they lowered their home price much more from the start, or employed Dick and Jane's $5,000-a-week-off method, they probably would have gotten out much sooner—and with a higher price.

Feeling at Peace With a Lower Price

Even if you completely agree with all the reasons for selling your property for a lesser amount and you decide to go ahead with it, something strange can happen: you can start feeling sorry for yourself and forget all the reasons why you lowered your price!

You might feel like you're cheating yourself, or you're not being a very good businessperson. This is especially true if you see other properties come on the market that are as nice as yours, but listed for higher amounts. (These people may not be as motivated, or at least not yet.)

You may also suffer from a delayed reaction: you feel at peace with a lower price while your property is on the market. But once it sells you begin wondering if you could have or should have asked for more. To prevent this from happening and eliminate the possibility of regret later on, write yourself a list of every possible reason you decided to sell your property at a lower price.

Here is an example of such a list:

1. I want to get out of my adjustable rate mortgage before it resets at a higher rate.
2. I want to sell before my next big property tax bill is due.
3. I want to reduce my monthly expenses.
4. I don't want to worry about higher utility prices down the line.
5. I'm tired of living in uncertainty, not knowing how long this housing slump may last.
6. I want to live closer to work.
7. I want to live within walking distance to the things I need.

8. I am tired of cleaning up my place in case someone comes by.
9. I want to move out before they start building an apartment complex across the street, which will bring non-stop construction noise and dust.
10. I want to get out of debt.
11. I want to be able to take a vacation and not worry about having my house shown while I am gone.
12. I want to move away from my crazy neighbor.
13. I want to move away from all the barking dogs in our neighborhood.
14. I want to move away from the hurricane belt.
15. I want to live in a nicer climate.
16. I want to move to a less crowded area.
17. I want to live in a better school district.
18. I want to live closer to my family.

Write down all the reasons you want to move away from where you are now and all the reasons you want to start a new life elsewhere. Write them all down, from your biggest concerns to your pettiest complaints. Then make sure to keep this list somewhere you can find it, so you can read it anytime you feel a pang of regret. Once you remember all the reasons why you're selling, or why you sold your house for less, you'll feel much wiser and better about making that decision.

When *Not* to Lower Your Price (or lower it any more than it is)

It's time for some good news: there are occasions when you might not want to or need to lower your property price. It depends on your individual situation and your particular piece of property. Here are some circumstances where you may choose to stick to your preferred asking price:

- You don't mind waiting until a great offer comes along. You're not under financial pressure, you enjoy living where you are, and it doesn't bother you to have people peeping through your closets for an extended period of time.

- You can hold out financially, and you've got a unique property with distinctive features that are hard to find. For example, if you've got a large workshop, a beautiful organic garden, a working greenhouse, a drop-dead ocean view, a tennis court, or a private boat dock, you may want to wait for the right buyer to come along. These features won't attract everyone, but the person who needs or wants what you have *might* be willing to pay your price for it. The beauty of having unique features such as these is that it can be easier to target specific types of buyers who may be interested in your property. You'll be hearing more about how to employ niche marketing in Chapter Ten, in the section called, "How To Get More People to Your Front Door."

- You might, in truth, not really want to sell your property. You may want to stay where you are, but because of financial or other reasons you feel the need to sell. In a case like this, by keeping your preferred asking price, you can buy yourself a little time to figure out what to do. If you decide you really do want or need to move, you can lower your asking price and increase your chance of a sale. But, if you decide you would rather stay, it gives you time to come up with creative financial solutions or arrangements that may keep you from having to leave.

- Your property has plunged in value and you'll lose all kinds of money if you sell quickly at a lower price. If you can hold out financially, it may make sense for you to keep your price where you want it, or take your house off the market until real estate is selling better. If by chance an offer comes in at your preferred price, you win! However, you should only keep your preferred asking price higher if you can afford to pay the bills and wait it out. Don't do this, however, if you think the market is going to remain slow for an extended period of time and you're putting yourself under ever-increasing financial pressure.

- If you're already asking an extremely low price and it still isn't selling, you might want to hold the line where you are now—IF you can handle it financially. This is especially true if the cost of selling your house, after subtracting commissions, closing costs, and moving costs will end up losing you a lot of money.

The Emotional Side of Setting Your Home Price

When it comes to pricing your home, it's easy to equate your home price with your price as a person. That's one of the reasons many people don't want to lower their price, even if it will help them sell their home more quickly. It might not be because they'll be underwater with their loan—it's because they don't want the price they identify themselves with to slip below a certain level.

Home sellers say to themselves, "I don't want to go below $300,000; I'm worth that!" The same thing goes with those asking $500,000 or $1,000,000. The million-dollar man or woman wants to stay that way. It's part of human nature. I felt this way when I had my home on the market too. When our agent recommended we lower the price to get more action, the voice in my head yelled, "Oh no, MY price is going down!"

It's important to realize we are not our home prices. If you go from $300,000 to $295,000, you won't look in the mirror and see less of yourself. All that happens is you might have more people knocking on your door because they're looking for a house under $300,000 right now. I know it stinks, but it works. In terms of your personal worth, you should pride yourself in knowing you're someone with enough self-esteem to *not* use your home price as a personal marker. In fact, if you end up selling your home quickly, you can feel good about yourself because you were responsible for changing your destiny. You lowered your price so you can move on with the next chapter in your life.

Of course, this doesn't apply to every home owner and every pricing situation, but those of you holding on to a certain price for personal reasons, you know who you are. If this is the case, you may want to ask yourself what hurts the most about lowering your home price. Is it because you'll be badly damaged financially, or is it because it will damage your identity? If it's for the second reason, the good news is you will get over it. I did. It turns out that self-esteem can be pretty resilient.

How Not To Be Stuck When You're Stuck

In the event that you can't sell your house quickly, whether it's because you don't want to lower your price or it's just not selling, it's good to know you have options. Here are a few ideas that people are using to weather the storm.

- Rent your home out to cover your expenses and move to a lower cost place. I know of a number of people who have successfully done this and significantly lowered their financial pressures. Many people who have rented their houses are moving to lower cost cities, or out of the United States to places such as Mexico, Thailand, and Central or South America where the cost of living is much lower. One couple I know rented out their home for $3,000 a month and moved to a little beach cottage in Mexico for $500 a month. Not only did they eliminate the problem of paying their monthly mortgage, they're also enjoying a new, more relaxed lifestyle.

- Consider doing a home exchange. There are two types of these. One type is to actually exchange ownership of the homes, the other is to do a temporary swap of living spaces only. The temporary swap can be a great solution when both parties are stuck with houses they can't sell and are itching to get out of town or have been temporarily transferred on business. You can swap your city condo for a cabin in the country, a house in the suburbs or even an ancient stone cottage in Italy. Of course you've got to be careful to whom you give your keys to, but there are many precautions you can take before trading places. If this sounds of interest, do an Internet search for "Home Exchange" or "House Swapping" to learn more about it.

- Rent out a portion of your house. If you want to stay where you are but want a little help covering your expenses, adding a roommate or roommates might ease your burden. My grandparents were big on having "boarders" in their home to help pay their expenses. As a kid I always remember my grandfather counting out the money brought in by these people who occupied their extra rooms. This was a Depression-era solution, but it seems to be coming back. You will of course want to get some references and do a credit and background check before letting them move in though.

· Rent out an unattached portion of your home. If you don't want someone living in your house, you may still be able to rent out a part of your property, such as a guest cottage, workshop, garage, or even a piece of your land. In this case, your renters might not be living with you, but using it for work or storage only. I know one man who rents out his extra garage space, and a woman who rents her neighbor's guesthouse to use as a massage therapy office. Another clever couple I know built a spacious room with almost nothing in it that they rent out as a meeting place. If you've got a big plot of land, you might rent out your dirt to someone who will grow vegetables on it. One word of warning though, before you go ahead and rent out your space: make sure your area is zoned for it. And it's a good idea to learn a little about whom you are renting to—you don't want someone using your garage to stack up dead bodies.

· If the idea of renting out space or taking a roommate doesn't appeal to you, there are thousands of side-businesses you can start from your home that can bring in extra income. You probably have a talent or two you can put to work for you. One woman I know became a minister and performed weddings every weekend. Another started an eBay business selling used books she found at garage sales. Or, you can become a tutor or a consultant, or produce "how to" videos on a topic that you know a lot about. Also consider what your friends need. Could they use a pet sitter? Someone to run errands? A closet organizer? There's one woman I know who has gone into business helping families sort through possessions left by departed relatives. She holds estate and garage sales and makes a nice living helping people who need her assistance. Any of these things can turn into a growing business just by offering your services to friends who end up referring you to others. We'll talk more about using your talents in Chapter Nine, in the section called "Reclarify Your Worth."

- Finally, there's the traditional approach: ask for a raise or a promotion, get a part-time job, or find a way to get paid to do something new for a business where you already work. Maybe you can start doing the catering for your company's events or take over the graphic design work that your company usually hires out.

By tapping into one or more of these solutions you can overcome financial issues, start new life adventures and meet new people who can open the door to more opportunities. So being stuck with a house that is hard to sell doesn't have to be the end of the world. In fact, it can be a new beginning.

Perspective Is Everything

"Things might look good, or things might look bad.
Either way you're right."—The Author

One of my greatest life lessons to date is that we are able to perceive the world from any side we choose, and we're free to shift our perspective any time we want.

When you see the state of the world, the economy or any other issue from a chosen perspective, it's natural to collect and recall all the information that confirms our existing viewpoint. For example, if you think the economy is in bad shape you'll take note of a dozen indicators that prove you're right: Housing prices are heading downward. Bankruptcies, foreclosures, personal debt and layoffs are increasing. Then there's the declining dollar, the growing deficit, the looming oil crisis, the health care crisis and high military expenses. Add to this, we are witnessing more turbulent weather patterns and weather-related disasters that are costing the country millions of dollars in damage and lost production every year. When you take all of this into consideration the economic forecast looks dismal. In an economy that shows all these indicators, it's easy to believe that selling a property is going to be difficult.

But at the exact same time, there is another group of people who hold a very different viewpoint. Rather than noticing and collecting all the bad news, they focus on the signs of abundance. They notice crowded restaurants, theaters and hotels—and see them all as signs that the economy is still alive. They take note of new businesses opening up, promising technological solutions that can solve some of the world's problems, and road construction and infrastructure projects bringing jobs and money into local areas.

As further indication that things are looking up, this group focuses on the fact that billions of dollars are flowing through people's hands every day. Businesses worldwide are still being bought and sold. Stocks, commodities and international currency are making money for people whether the markets are going up or down. And when the U.S. dollar declines, it means that international markets can buy U.S. products (and properties) for less, because other currencies are worth more.

In fact, U.S. properties can be especially attractive to

people from other countries because they benefit in two ways: being able to buy properties for lower prices due to the slow housing market, and the ability to buy more property per dollar because of the dollar's lower value. Some feel this alone might help keep U.S. property prices from sinking lower and lower.

In addition, millions of Baby Boomers are inheriting their parent's assets, leading to the largest transfer of intergenerational wealth in the history of mankind.

Adding this all up, a person can come to the conclusion that there's plenty of money available to buy property— including yours!

So, as you see, you can view the world very differently based on your chosen viewpoint. This doesn't mean you should abandon your life-long beliefs this very moment, but it's freeing to realize you have the power to choose and balance your perspective. In so doing, it gives you the power to make important decisions, such as whether to lower your property price or not, based on knowledge gathered from both sides of the coin.

One Person's White Elephant is Another's Perfect Castle

Here's a true story of two people's different perspectives in action:

Barbara owned a 5-bedroom two-story home in a town with a large retiree population. Even though the housing market was slow, she decided to put her house up for sale because she wanted to move to Hawaii.

The day her "For Sale" sign went up, Barbara's neighbor Marcy came running over and announced that it was a terrible time to try and sell her house. "No one is buying!" she said, "and on top of that, the older people who are moving to this area don't want a house with stairs, especially a large house that requires so much upkeep!" Marcy urged Barbara to wait until the market picked back up before trying to sell. (In actuality, Marcy was concerned that Barbara would have to sell her house at a greatly reduced price, which would lower the market price even more in their neighborhood.)

But Barbara had her heart set on moving to Hawaii and kept her house on the market even though she thoroughly understood Marcy's viewpoint. Within two months Barbara found a buyer, which turned out to be two 30-something sisters and their husbands. The two couples had been searching high and low for a large two-story house where they could split expenses, be out of each other's hair, but live close to where they all worked.

Barbara's house was perfect because there were hardly any two-story houses in the neighborhood, due to the high concentration of retirees who had built smaller, single-level homes there.

When Marcy found out that Barbara sold her home so quickly she was shocked and told her she was incredibly lucky. But Barbara didn't see it that way. She had held a different perspective, one in which she knew her house would be the perfect fit for someone, and she was right. Again, this is why it pays to shift your perspective and look at both sides of the coin when making a major selling decision.

Even If You Make A Bad Decision—It Can Still Turn Out Well

To further complicate how we see things, we can even question what it means to make a good decision versus a bad one. That's because within many good decisions there is still a downside, and behind our bad decisions there can be an upside.

For example, one couple I know decided to go on their dream vacation: a month-long safari trip to Africa. On that trip they had some of the best, most memorable times in their lives. They saw all of the wild animals they had always wanted to see and they created multiple stunning photo albums, which they enjoyed revisiting frequently. However, to take this trip, they ended up spending money they had been thinking of using to expand their catering company. As a result, it took them longer to grow their business. So, even though their safari was a great success, it did have its downside.

There is a little exercise that fully illustrates this point. I've often used it with business consulting clients who are feeling stuck and afraid to make a decision in case they make the wrong choice.

This is how the exercise works:
Take out a piece of paper and on the left side of the page list some of the good decisions you've made in your life. Then on the right side, list some of your not-so-good decisions. (Notice, I didn't say "bad decisions." That sounds too harsh.) Now look at each decision, good and not-so-good, and consider the outcomes of each.

What you'll see is that even the best decisions most likely caused you to give something up, and the not-so-good decisions still brought you some nice consequences. For example, take my business-consulting client, Bob. Under his list of "not-so-good" decisions, he listed a job he took which ended up leading to a dead-end path in his career. But, simultaneously he realized while doing this exercise how many good things came out of it. He learned a lot about marketing and business management—which turned out to be a huge factor in his later success when he formed his own company. Plus, he met some people at his dead-end job who played a major role in supporting him in his new business.

Had Bob not taken that bad job, he may not have succeeded to the degree he did when he went out on his own. Once Bob realized that even his bad decisions often have good consequences, he became a little more relaxed about making decisions. It was just a matter of changing his perspective to see that.

The same goes with the decision you make about selling your property:

- If you decide to lower your price, you increase your chance of getting a buyer's attention, which can help you sell sooner, get out of debt if you're in it, and start a new life.
- If you don't lower your price (and can afford to stick it out), you don't have to feel as if you're giving your house away too cheaply. You'll have more time to pack up for a move if it takes longer to sell, and it gives you extra time to do some of the enjoyable things in your area that you haven't gotten around to doing yet. Plus, after months of practice you can get in the habit of keeping your home clean and organized while it's on the market.
- If you take your house off the market, you don't have to worry about keeping your home perfectly clean, you don't have to sell it for less, you don't have to worry about the logistics, stress and expense of moving, and you can enjoy the stability of living in the same community. Instead, you can put your energy into exploring new endeavors right

where you are. Then, when the housing market picks back up, you can jump back in if you decide you want to sell.

As you can see, there are three choices and all of them can be winners. So pick the one that makes the most financial and emotional sense to you and make peace with it.

What you *don't* want to do, however, is to make a decision and then spend all of your time wondering if you should have made another decision. Or, spend your time focusing only on the negative aspects of the decision you made. I find that usually what's more important than the decisions you make— is making whatever decision you make—work for you.

CHAPTER THREE

Making Your Home Stand Out in a Buyer's Mind

Because buyers have so many choices, when they walk through a home they categorize it into one of three groups:

- Properties they immediately like and put on their short list of possible buys.
- Properties they immediately dislike and forget.
- Properties that fall in the middle, which are lumped together with other so-so properties and probably soon forgotten.

The Red and Green Checkmark Game

In order to categorize your home, buyers—whether they know it or not—use a mental checkmark system. When they see a feature they like, they give it a symbolic green checkmark. (They might even take notes or photos.) When they see something unappealing or that doesn't fit with what they are looking for, they give it a red checkmark. In this way, buyers create a running tally of checkmarks for (or against) buying your property. The property that gets the most green checkmarks wins.

Your mission as a seller is to eliminate as many red checkmarks as you can, while filling the buyer's mind with as many green checkmarks as possible.

Here's what the buyer's internal dialogue sounds like:

Ooooh, nice entrance . . . (green checkmark)

Oh-oh, ugly crowded living room . . . (red checkmark)

Great view of the garden from the dining room . . . (green checkmark)

Yuck. The walls are too dark in the bedroom . . . (red checkmark)

Hmmm . . . there's a musty smell in the den . . . (red checkmark)

Nice patio for outside dining . . . (green checkmark)

Do I want to buy it? Probably not. Let's go see the next one.

In this dialog, you have just witnessed a house hunter lump this property into the so-so category where it will probably be forgotten, even though it received a number of green checkmarks.

It's also important to note that all it takes is one big red checkmark to potentially knock you out of the running. You might have a nice house with lots of great features, but all it takes is a smelly carpet or one big dead bug on the doorstep to outweigh everything else. The buyer may remember those red checkmarks more than your new French doors or polished nickel faucets. So you've got to look at your own property through the mind of a buyer, searching out possible green and red checkmarks as you roam from room to room.

In the next section we'll cover many fast, simple strategies that will maximize the number of green checkmarks you get, while eliminating the red ones.

Home Staging the Easy Way (Without paying big bucks)

You've probably heard of the term home staging before and know it entails making your property look better so you can sell it faster and get the most money for it. In a buyers' market this is even more important because your competition is doing the same thing.

Some home sellers spend a lot of money bringing in professional home stagers to give their place a facelift. Others buy colorful picture books showing photos of rooms that are well staged, and then try to duplicate the look by bringing in new pieces of furniture and accessories. But I think the best way to learn how to stage your home is to understand the principles behind what makes a home look irresistible to buyers, so you can do it yourself.

It's not about the quality of the fabric covering your sofas and windows, or whether to have an odd number of satin pillows stacked on your bed—what's more important is knowing the little secrets behind what makes a person walk into your place and never want to leave.

Once you understand the principles, you don't have to follow exact recipes or spend a lot of money bringing in new things. You can use your unique creativity along with things you already own (or can buy for cheap) to create a wonderfully staged, memorable home environment.

First we'll start with the big principles and then we'll go

into the individual touches that will stand out in a buyer's mind.

▪ Keep It Clean, Clean, Clean

This is probably obvious and a little boring, but it can't be overstated. House hunters are *not* attracted to dirt. Before you put your house on the market make it a clean machine. Get your carpets professionally cleaned and scrub your tiles, counters, sinks, toilets, showers and floors. Wash your windows, clean the blinds, dry clean the curtains and sweep anywhere that dust or cobwebs collect. If you were to do any one thing to your home to make it more sellable, this is it.

It seems that people have a supernatural ability to feel where dirt is, so don't try to ignore dirty corners or hide messes behind a piece of furniture or planter. Many home-buyers will sense they are there. Your best bet is to tackle these messes head-on and get rid of them so your place is truly clean.

▪ Create a Fantasy

The best way to get home buyers to establish an emotional connection to your home is to make them feel happy being there. You want people to see themselves living the good life within your walls.

The artist Thomas McKnight is a master of creating images of comfortable home interiors and terraces in beautiful locations. To see examples of his work, visit http://www.prints. com and look at McKnight's paintings of homes all over the world. Many of his images include cozy sitting places, cushy pillows, woven rugs, stacks of inviting books, vases brimming with flowers, open windows and baskets of fruit just waiting to be eaten. (Some images even include decorative napkins to help you imagine serving yourself.)

Each work is a homey fantasy that makes us want to jump in and pretend that we own the place. What makes these images even better is that there is no one else around. McKnight typically leaves people out of his scenes so that you can more easily fantasize coming in and seating yourself in one of his vacant chairs. This is the essence of staging.

Even though McKnight's images usually depict expensive homes with million-dollar views, we can create a similar feeling in our own homes. Maybe you don't have a sweeping view of New York's Central Park or Italy's Amalfi coastline, but you can put a birdbath or pots of flowers outside of your window to create a relaxing setting. And it's pretty quick and easy to create cozy sitting places using a basket of fruit, a woven rug and a stack of books. (You can even throw in some decorative napkins.) Once you do this, you'll enjoy living in your home even more while awaiting a sale.

▪ Make Your Home Anonymous

When prospects walk through your home, they want to be able to imagine themselves living within your walls. If they feel as if they've just walked in on your personal life, they can't do that. So while your house is on the market, try to make it as easy as possible for house hunters to superimpose their own lives in your living space.

Take down the photos of you, your wedding, your grandparents, and your honeymoon in Paris. Even though these photos represent the happiness of the people who live in your home, they make buyers feel out of place and less comfortable. People want to imagine their own life story in your house, not yours.

When people feel like they've intruded in your personal space, they want to get out more quickly. This of course, is exactly what you don't want. You want potential buyers to give your house a fair chance. You want them to grow an emotional attachment to your place so they'll think seriously about buying it.

Also, no offense, but remove any signposts of your unique hobbies, inclinations, and political and religious views. If buyers don't like the things you do, or what you believe in, they'll transfer their feelings to your house. So stash any rabid political books, hunting trophies, taxidermy projects and tarot card decks. Instead think like Thomas McKnight and make your home look like a scene that anyone would want to step into and relax.

Another way to look at this is to imagine that you're a detective looking for personal clues about your life. What would you hide to make your house look anonymous? That's the same stuff you want to hide to appeal to the widest possible audience of buyers.

▪ Make Your Home A Vacuum (But less noisy)

You've probably heard the old quote, "Nature abhors a vacuum." Well, this applies to the home you are trying to sell as well. If your home has empty space and breathing room, it's easier for buyers to imagine moving themselves and their possessions into your surroundings. But, if almost every square foot of your space is occupied, a buyer will feel crowded out.

An easy formula to follow is to try and remove about 50% of everything that is in plain sight, as well as 50% of the things you've got crushed into your closet and shelves. (Buyers might peek.) If there is space between the hangers in your closet, the cups in your cupboard, and the toiletries on your bathroom counter, people will be able to envision themselves unpacking their own things and making themselves at home.

Based upon this, you'd think that leaving your house totally empty would be the best scenario, because it gives people an empty canvas in which to add their lives. However, leaving too much empty space isn't a good thing either. A house devoid of furnishings, with big blank walls, feels too cold. Often people can't imagine how to arrange their furniture in your rooms and they can't judge the size of the room if it's completely bare. That's one of the reasons new housing developments provide furnished models.

If you have a hard time motivating yourself to create some empty space, just pretend your favorite sexy movie star is moving in for a couple of months and you want them to feel at home by making space for their things. A potential buyer will appreciate this just as much.

■ Make Your Home Appear Carefree

One of the simple things you can do to make your home look more inviting is to hide all the signs of your typical, non-carefree life. That's one of the reasons you don't see a stack of bills, a dust mop, or a bottle of aspirin in Thomas McKnight's fantasy room images.

If the environment feels calm and relaxed, buyers might start feeling that way themselves, and think that if they moved into your home they can embark on a happier, less stressful life chapter.

This means you've got to hide items such as newspapers and magazines with bad news on the cover, parking tickets, jury duty notices, bandages, cold medicine, eye drops, weed killer and fly swatters.

You also want to get rid of everyday signs of struggle over dirt and chaos. That means hiding your vacuum cleaner, wet sponges, dirty dishes, toilet plunger and any fallen hairs in your bathroom sink. When your place looks clean and organized, with no sign of these tidbits in sight, it gives the impression that peace and orderliness come easy in your environment.

▪ Make Your View Stand Out

Every professional home stager knows the importance of emphasizing a home's view. If you have a room with a view of the rolling hills, a lake, a cityscape, or even a grand old tree, rather than clutter up your interior with heavy distracting furniture and decorations, it's often better to turn buyers' eyes to the beautiful view outside.

This means making the room itself act as a frame for the outdoor surroundings. This is much like a woman who wears a simple black dress, so that the attention is drawn to her face or figure, rather than the fabric and patterns she wears.

The good news about this is you don't have to spend a lot of money and resources fancying up the interior décor. Quite often muted furnishings and hushed wall colors will serve you best. Just keep the room clean, uncluttered and arrange your furniture so the views are your centerpiece.

However, if your external views are nothing to write home about—for example, if you face a parking lot, a row of dumpsters or a cement wall—don't abandon hope. Instead of leading the eye outside, direct the buyer's attention toward a central interior focal point, such as a piece of art or a relaxing sitting area.

One smart decorator, whose condo features a gorgeous view of a parking lot, shifted the focal point from what was outside her window to what was in front of it. She brought in a large marble pedestal and a sculpture of the Greek goddess Diana. Then she hung luxurious gold drapes over her windows and artfully lit the whole scene with accent lights. Wow! No one thinks to look outside at the row of cars when they enter her room.

■ Make Every Room a Hang-Out Spot

It's not difficult to make every room in your home look like a worthwhile destination. Your living room can resemble a lovely hotel lobby, your kitchen—an attractive restaurant, your bathroom—a luxurious guest spa, and even your laundry room can become worthy of a couple of ooohs and ahhhhs.

By doing so, you'll make potential buyers feel like staying longer and soaking up the ambiance. During my own home selling experiences, I can often judge the success of a showing if there is a "butt print" left on my cushy sofa. This subtle piece of evidence tells me that someone liked my house enough to want to sit down and stay a bit. (Either that or they were just very tired.) The nice thing about creating such an environment is that even though your goal is to sell, you get a chance to enjoy your place at its very best while you're still there.

Here are some examples of how to make each room in your

house a worthwhile destination. It doesn't matter whether your home is a villa on the Isle of Capri or a double-wide on a dirt lane, here's how to make your home worthy of having someone want to plant a "butt print" on your sofa.

▪ The Kitchen and Dining Room

Aim to make your kitchen and dining room feel like a welcoming restaurant, whether it's a French Café, a cute 1960's diner, a country kitchen or an Italian Bistro. To get you in the mood, close your eyes and imagine what you would see if you entered one of these places. What would it look like? Hint: you probably wouldn't see a wrinkled bag of chips, a plastic bin of old potatoes, or a pile of mail.

What you would see is a clean table ready and waiting, a little vase of flowers perhaps, and welcoming chairs free of crumbs. You'd also see clean counters, uncluttered floors and interesting artwork on the walls. This is the kind of place that makes you feel like coming in and sitting down. Depending upon the look you are going for, you can set the stage by dressing up the table with a nice tablecloth or placemats along with dishes, stemware, or simple cheery teacups.

Add some decorative touches to your countertops, such as a bright bowl of lemons, a bottle of wine and a corkscrew, a cheese board and knife, or one of those tall glass containers filled with layers of red and green peppers or olives. These artful containers make your kitchen look quite gourmet, and once your house sells you can celebrate by eating up the contents. (As long as it doesn't take too many years to sell your house.)

Use your walls to display decorations and kitchen tools that go along with your dining theme. You can get incredibly creative using everyday items such as a hanging spice rack, a shelf full of cookbooks or a collection of attractive aprons hanging in a row. One couple I knew hung framed menus from all their local eateries. This turned out to be a great conversation piece and an inexpensive way to brighten up their kitchen.

You can also hang a wooden or metal ceiling rack above your stove, center island, breakfast bar or counter top. Then use hooks to hang attractive pots and pans, utensils, or even dried flowers or bunches of herbs. The rack not only adds charm, it can serve as a subtle room divider between the kitchen and dining area.

The bottom line is you want people to walk into your eating rooms and see themselves happily cooking, dining and enjoying time spent with their family and friends. By coming up with a particular theme, such as a French café, you'll make your kitchen feel even more like a welcoming restaurant.

▪ The Living Room

Aim to make your living room feel like a welcoming hotel lobby or suite. Again, make it a place where there is breathing room. Don't stuff the room full of furniture, knick-knacks and family photos.

Leave open space on your coffee table, end tables and book shelves. By cluttering up these areas with newspapers, magazines and remote controls you can stress out homebuyers because they pick up on the fact that you probably don't do that much relaxing there.

To make your living room more livable, showcase only your most prized, beautiful or interesting items. For example, the coffee table can display a bowl of fruit, a vase of flowers, a couple of beautiful books, and that's it.

Don't give in to the temptation of relocating your cluttered items from another room (such as your entryway) into your living room either. And don't try to hide a pile of something in a corner. People can feel cluttered energy. It's like knowing someone is hiding in the closet. Instead, do the opposite—accentuate your bare areas.

Pick a color scheme or theme to pull the room together. If you've got a few interesting items hanging around, such as southwestern or modern art pieces you can work your room around the colors or theme of your art. For example, if you've got an interesting wooden sailing ship model, bring in a couple of other similar items to go along with it and take away the decorations that get in the way of your theme.

Don't worry about not having a room full of new, expensive furniture—there are ways around this. If your sofa or chairs look old and beat, get slipcovers to hide their age. If you don't want to pay for new slipcovers, use king-size woven "sweater" blankets to hide your older pieces. Add a few decorative pillows and you can have a whole new look in any color you want.

I can't tell you how much mileage I've gotten out of this idea alone. For example, I've got a green chaise lounge that I bought from a mail order catalog that looked stunning in the photo, but when I unpacked it from the box it looked old and ugly from day one. But this chaise was tremendously comfortable and I instantly enjoyed kicking back and reading in it, so I didn't want to return it.

Instead, I hid the thing under a $14.99 off-white woven

blanket, tossed in a few sparkling accent pillows and I had a luxurious lounging area. Over the years this chaise has moved from house to house and from room to room, each time blending in with a new color scheme and theme. You can do this same magic to many sitting surfaces in your house!

The next step is to throw in a few expensive-looking items to upgrade the whole feel of the living room. For example, bring in an iron statue or a sculpture from a home décor store as a focal point. This is the equivalent of wearing jeans and a T-shirt, but sporting an expensive-looking piece of jewelry or belt that keeps them all guessing.

You can find some attractive, sculptures at places such as Pier One, World Market, or at internationally themed bazaar stores. Often one or two pieces like this can give the whole room a richer look.

The other aspect of your living room to consider is your windows. If you've got a great view, good weather and an absence of honking, screaming and exhaust fumes, keep your windows open and let the sunshine and bird song in. Frame your windows with pleasant, easy to open window treatments. Get rid of any old curtains or dysfunctional blinds and replace them with breezy sheers or light cotton panels that fit your particular room.

You can outfit your windows at Target or Costco and no one will ever know. If you've got your own sewing machine, (or know someone who does) you can even take some plain nice sheets and make them into new curtains.

Put it all together and you've created a worthy destination where homebuyers can see themselves living in your living room.

▪ The Bedroom

Although you may have more than one bedroom, let's focus on the master bedroom. Here, you want to aim for making your room look like a nice, calming hotel room. And I do mean hotel room, not motel room, so stay away from the ugly polyester flowery bedspreads and old fake-wood, brown dresser units.

You want to create a bedroom where strangers would feel comfortable entering, even though they don't know you. The less personal stuff and clutter showing, the better. Stash away your slippers, bathrobe, and antacids, because they make people want to flee. Also, hide your stuffed animals. As cute as they may be, they make your bedroom look too personal. You wouldn't find them in a nice hotel room, so don't put them on display here either. (Unless you're talking about a children's room of course.)

Your goal, as always, is to enable potential buyers to see themselves in your personal space. If the room screams YOU, buyers can't take the leap of imagination to see themselves hanging up their bathrobe next to yours.

So keep the master bedroom simple: a bed, a nightstand, a chest, a chair, a lamp and a mirror are really all you need. Add some clean curtains, a rug perhaps, a trunk if you need to store things, one or two paintings—and you're done.

For bonus points pick a theme and work around it. Throw in a few decorative items that give your room a cheerful feel and leave plenty of clean, dusted, empty space everywhere else, just like a hotel room. Luckily you don't have to put out room service menus or hang up signs indicating where the emergency exits are. In fact, if you're really lucky, the buyers won't think of exiting at all. Instead they'll think about moving in.

■ The Bathroom

Ultimately, you want your bathroom to look like a resort health spa. Okay, maybe a very tiny resort health spa. Even if your bathroom is three-by-four feet, it doesn't take much to achieve the spa look.

First, hide all the usual suspects that take the beauty and serenity out of a bathroom, such as the automatic toothbrush, gummy toothpaste tubes, splintering soap bars, dental floss, skin creams, shaving gear, used towels and bottles of vitamins. Also hide your cleaning supplies such as sponges, scrubbers and plungers.

Now look at the color on your walls. If they look dull, think about painting them a soft, calming color such as moss green, pale yellow or peach. Since bathrooms are usually small, they shouldn't take long to paint, and simply adding color can make a big difference.

If your floors aren't attractive, throw down a plush, colorful rug to draw attention away from the flooring. Select a rug color that works well with your wall color, and then bring in towels, curtains, and a matching shower curtain, rods and hooks to match or complement your color scheme.

If you have old faucets, towel racks, or lighting fixtures, consider replacing them with newer, attractive accessories. If you want to add a little more of an "ahhh" factor, install one of the large spa-sized showerheads with a million holes that look like a sunflower. (But don't be shocked if you come home and find a naked stranger taking a shower in your little resort spa.)

You can purchase all of these inexpensively, and they might

make a big difference between a boring, non-memorable bathroom and a bath that looks like a calming little oasis. What makes it even better is that these home improvements can be done quickly on your own.

Now all you need to do is add a few welcoming accents. Place a glass jar filled with pastel soaps on your countertop, roll up a few fluffy towels in a wicker basket, and hang a decorative knob on the wall for placing your clothes while showering. However, don't instantly hang your own things on it. Keep it vacant so that people can imagine hanging their own clothes on it.

Finally, hang up a few photos or little paintings on your walls, such as a beautiful forest, a meadow, a beach scene, or a close up of a flower. A very inexpensive way to find great bathroom art is to buy some nature photography greeting cards and pop them inside 5" x 7" frames or plastic frame boxes. Tah-dah! You've got instant spa art!

Just be careful to choose images that are appropriate for a bathroom. When my parents were getting ready to put their home on the market, my mother asked my dad to hang a picture of something beautiful on the wall behind the toilet. She was not delighted to find he had hung up a still-life painting of a cutting board overflowing with fruit and cheese. Somehow foodie pictures just don't belong in a bathroom.

▪ The Home Office or Study

If you have a home office, the main thing you want to do is keep it clean and organized. If you turn your back for just a few days, you know what can happen: piles of papers, coffee cups, files, sticky notes and other miscellaneous items start to accumulate. Even your office trash will try to take over.

None of these things make potential homebuyers feel like setting up shop in this room. If they walk into an office where chaos reins supreme, they'll start to feel your stress, which completely undermines the goal of creating the appearance of a "carefree" environment. Remember, you want to make buyers imagine that if they lived in your lovely home and worked in your organized office, somehow their own lives would become equally organized and lovely. (Do I hear you laughing?)

To achieve this look means keeping your work surfaces clean and uncluttered, hiding your paper piles in file cabinets, drawers or boxes, and tucking away any tangled nests of power cords. Your stapler, tape, paper clips, pens and stationery should have an attractive little home, and dust bunnies should not roll across your desktop. You should also keep your keyboard free of crumbs and grime, which might give away the fact that you spend a great deal of your time eating and living in front of your computer.

Because this room is all about function, you don't need to worry so much about finding attractive furnishings, peripherals and desk accessories. You can have boxes of files on a card table without offending most people. So don't worry about spending money in this room. If you want to put any money into a room, go for the kitchen and baths instead.

▪ The Laundry Room

You might not think you can do much to a laundry room, but actually you can have a lot of fun in here. With a little creativity and some quick touches, you can transform this room from a dull box with a washer and dryer into a sweet room that house hunters will remember.

What can you do to a laundry room? First, show off the room's cleanliness and functionality. Add an empty wicker basket for clean laundry and put attractive bottles of cleaning solutions on your countertop. Nowadays you can find stylish bottles of scented goops in gourmet kitchen shops, health food stores, or even at your local market.

Choose a color theme for your walls—and it definitely doesn't have to be white. If your washer and dryer are in the way, just paint one or two walls a different accent color. This color can then serve as the theme for your cleaner bottles and other decorative touches. You can also add a stenciled or paper border around the entire perimeter of your walls.

It's amazing what a few little accents can do for this room. I had one laundry room that started out as just a white square with white plywood drawers and cabinets and a grey plastic countertop. In one weekend I was able to transform it.

First, I painted the room a bold cornflower blue, which looked great against the white washer and dryer, and even accentuated the blue dials and buttons. Then I added a stick-on boarder all the way around the top of the room. The border featured a clothesline hung with blue jeans flying in the wind, which matched the walls perfectly.

Next, I changed the cabinet and drawer pulls from plain white to ceramic blue checkerboard knobs. Then I hung some matching checkerboard hooks and hangers for clothes along with some greeting cards of blue birds in picture frames. I also got a new white ceramic light switch plate and painted some blue flowers on it. For the finishing touch, I put a blue ribbon around a white wicker basket and filled it with different attractive bottles of blue-themed cleansers.

Amazing what a difference a color scheme did to this room!

It went from being the most boring room in the house to being one of the most interesting. And, being that the laundry room is one of those rooms where people end up spending a bit of time, you might as well make it as enjoyable as possible. If you do, buyers will imagine themselves doing their laundry and being pretty happy about it.

■ The Garage

You might not think that there's much you can do with a garage, but even this space can be made into a paradise. In fact, you can make your garage into a combination workshop, parking place and drive-in art gallery with little effort. (Depending on your garage's current degree of clutter or cleanliness.)

This room is your opportunity to strongly attract the male species, which is often drawn to garages and workshops like hummingbirds to a feeder. So let me give you a vision of the perfect he-man (or she-woman) haven, starting with organization.

All of the miscellaneous things in your garage can be placed in large, identically-sized plastic containers that are stacked on garage shelf units. Each is labeled with its contents for camping, car cleaning, crafts, gardening tools and hardware. The larger items are placed in bigger bins on the floor, or placed in a tall standing cabinet. (Note the strategic absence of tilting stacks of buckling old boxes in uneven sizes.)

If you have a small amount of extra space that isn't occupied by a car, you can assign the spot as a work area. Depending upon what this means to you, you could create a space for gardening by adding a potting bench and yard supplies, or you could create a woodwork station, an arts and crafts center, or a do-it-yourself home improvement area.

If you have a little more extra space, you can get an old door, prop it up on a couple of inexpensive cabinets or saw horses for support, and you've got a highly useful surface area. Bring in a chair and a shelf for your hobby books and you've created the perfect place to hide from domestic squabbles. (That goes for both men and women of course.)

In terms of your garage floor, it should be clean and swept free of dried leaves, dead bugs and spilled potting soil. If you've got oil stains on your floor that won't come out, there's even a solution for that. You can paint your floor with a concrete color wash that blends in with your current oil stains. These color washes are available at home centers and hardware stores and they come in a variety of colors including terra cotta, brick red, and different shades of brown and beige. Although these washes are usually used to give grey concrete patios and driveways a richer look, you can use them to beautify your garage floor and make a dramatic difference. I've even seen some garage floors done with a faux finish and a glossy overcoat, which almost makes the place look like a ballroom. (Make sure to read the directions on the can of stain before attempting to create such a ballroom.)

Now for the walls . . . White paint is just fine. Just keep the surfaces clean and get rid of the spider webs. If you really want your garage to stand out, hang some large framed pieces of artwork on your walls. Car photos always work well, as do photos of planes, bridges, buildings or gardens. This makes homebuyers fantasize. How often do they get to drive up into their own private art gallery? Even though you'll probably take your pictures with you when you move out, buyers see what is possible to create in this usually dull room.

One last thing to mention: consider the smell of your garage. If it smells like a gas station or auto shop, there are a couple of things you can do about that.

First, you can bring in zeolite rocks, which are little chemical-absorbing rocks that you can purchase in open-weave mesh bags that rid the air of petrochemical fumes and other odors. Just put the bags around your garage (do not open them) and let zeolite do the air cleaning. You can purchase these bags of wonder rocks online through companies such as www.allergystore.com, or do an Internet search on the topic to find out more about them.

Second, if your garage has a window with access to sunlight, you can bring in some houseplants. They not only beautify the space, they'll also absorb carbon dioxide and petrochemicals to improve your air quality. Put it all together and you've got a garage that people will remember—organized, artistic and functional all at the same time.

CHAPTER FOUR

Tricks and Touches to Make People Oooh and Ahhh

In this section you'll discover many simple tricks and inexpensive touches that will work on any kind of property and in many types of rooms, whether you've got a colonial mansion, an urban condo or a tract home in the suburbs. You don't need to remodel, you don't need to hire experts, and you don't need to spend a lot of money on décor.

Here are a number of simple things you can do to get as many green checkmarks as possible so your home ranks high in a buyer's mind.

■ Create Room Themes

If you think about successful stores, restaurants and resorts, you'll notice that they almost always have a theme. The places that don't have a theme are often fairly boring and utilitarian. Think of an office-building cafeteria versus an Italian bistro. Office cafeterias are usually devoid of themes and are pretty boring places to hang out. Now imagine an Italian bistro—here's a place you'd be happy to spend an hour or two nibbling, sipping, and talking. Even though they both offer you a bowl of soup and a table and chairs, the office cafeteria is easy to leave while the Italian bistro beckons you to stay and enjoy.

Themes don't have to be complicated either. They can be as simple as a color scheme carried throughout a room. For example, you can create a black, white and red theme to make a room look bolder and more exciting. That doesn't mean you have to buy all black, white and red furniture either. You can keep, for example, your brown wooden furniture and beige fabrics, but add black, white and red touches in your artwork, pillows, rugs, curtains or other accessories.

A theme can also bring to mind a place, era, or a style. One time I quickly transformed a small white room into a French colonial jungle-themed office by doing just a few simple steps. I painted the walls blue-green, brought in some palm-like house plants in woven baskets, hung up inexpensive wooden roll-up window shades and put an elephant statue in the corner. For the final touch, I bought a leopard spotted velour-covered trunk from a thrift store to serve as a file cabinet. Indeed it looked pretty tacky in the store, but it fit perfectly well in the midst of a jungle-themed office. The total cost for this makeover? $200.

One woman I know decided on a white and gold theme. This was easy for her, since she had a white rug, white walls and a white desk to begin with. She thought white was very soothing so she kept on going. She spray-painted her file cabinet white and brought in a couple of white chairs. Then as an accent, she brought in a few gold things such as a gold lamp, gold picture frames and an ultra-modern tall gold vase. The place looked fantastic—and very opulent. Again, it cost her very little to tie this all together.

The list of possible themes is endless. You can have a tropical theme, a Vegas theme, a sports theme, a 60's theme, a movie theme, an India theme, an Asian theme, a Western theme, an old Mexico theme, a Victorian theme, a floral theme, a Cape Cod theme, and that's just a start.

To get started, just look around your house at the items you've already collected. Do you have a lot of yellow things or ocean related items? If you do, you've got a theme in the making. Turn this into an enjoyable game with the end result being a room that is much easier to remember. Attractive, simple themes equate to green checkmarks in a house hunter's mind.

▪ Prevent Plain with Paint

Although real estate agents, decorators and stagers often recommend painting all the rooms in your house white or a neutral color to appeal to the largest pool of buyers, there is another side to the story. If you want your home to be noticed, you can't make it look like everyone else's place. If you do, at the end of a day of house hunting what will people remember? Probably not much. It will blend in with all the other neutral houses.

Besides from not standing out from the competition, many people have a hard time imagining a room looking any other way than it does right now. So if the walls look boring now, that's the way people will imagine them looking when they move their own furniture in.

In addition, there are a lot of people who are scared of paint. They're afraid to slash a bold stroke of peach or green across their wall to begin the painting process. However, if the wall is already a beautiful color, they aren't frightened of it.

Handing people a house with white walls is a lot like giving them a blank white canvas instead of a finished painting. Most people would rather choose the attractive finished painting than pick up a brush and try their own luck. However, this doesn't mean you should go ahead and indiscriminately paint all of your rooms bold colors just so your home will stand out. That could even lead to earning red checkmarks. But colors applied appropriately can earn you some positive points.

In addition to making your walls look better, color also unites everything in a room so your furniture and accessories look as if they belong together. If you've ever seen "before" and "after" photos of rooms that are exactly the same, except the colors of the walls have changed, then you know what I mean.

In the "before" photo where the walls are white, everything in the room seems to be floating on its own. The items just happen to be stuck in the room together. There's a couch here, a table there, a lamp in the corner and so on.

Then you look at the "after" photos where the walls have been painted a dramatic color, such as copper orange. Suddenly every item in the room looks tied together as a cohesive whole. The color of the couch ties in with the candleholders, which tie in with the rug and the framed art prints. All of these pieces suddenly pop out and the room looks gorgeous.

You can also paint various walls in the same room different colors. One wall might be bold while the others are a quieter shade of the same color. Or, use a stencil to paint on a design (such as a leaf, or flowers, or diamonds) in a second color. There are hundreds of stencil designs to choose from at art supply shops and home improvement stores, or you can even make your own stencil using cardboard.

In the book *Paint Can*, by Sunny Goode, you can see all sorts of wild and innovative paint treatments. You can paint your walls two different colors of wide alternating stripes; you can lay out a checkerboard of several colors on a wall, or even paint a room with color themed polka dots.

If you want to switch paint colors between rooms, or even on different walls within the same room without having a typical vertical dividing line where the two colors meet, you can extend one wall color onto the wall of a different color.

For example, let's say you want your living room to be green and your hallway yellow. Rather than have a hard vertical line where the green and yellow walls meet, you can wrap a little of the green living room color into the yellow hallway and wrap a little of the yellow hallway color into the living room. This can be done by painting a diagonal area of the first color in the upper or lower corner of the wall of the second color. (To help you do this, first draw a very light pencil line where you want the diagonal stripe to go.)

To keep the two colors from meeting and blending during the painting process, lay down some blue painter's tape along the diagonal pencil line. Then paint the two colors on opposite sides of the tape. When the paint dries, lift up the tape and you'll have two neat lines, accented by whatever third color was under the painter's tape. (White is often the best third color because it's neutral and it accentuates the other two colors.) This painting effect is guaranteed to earn you some ooooh and ahhhhs. It looks great and it's actually pretty easy to do.

I know a number of people who consider painting rooms good therapy. It's one of the fastest ways to feel like you've accomplished something big, but costs only a little. And, if you decide you don't like the wall colors you've chosen, you can always repaint them.

■ Write On Your Walls

I know, you were taught as a kid not to write on the walls, but these days the written word, creatively placed on the walls of your home, has been elevated to an art form. Leaders in the home decorating industry say that "interior typography," as it's officially called, is soaring to an all-time high.

Imagine walking into a kitchen, and there on the wall, in graceful scroll lettering, is the word, "Enjoy" or "Gourmet" or "Chocolate!" Or, walk into a bedroom and you see the word "Breathe" in antique gold lettering. Or, upon entering a home office, there above the desk is the perfectly placed word, "Create!" Any room of the house is worthy of a word, a quote, or a beautiful thought to remember.

Watch out for using phrases that personalize your space too much though. It's best to avoid phrases such as "Good morning Nancy!" or "I love ice fishing!" which buyers may not be able to identify with. Remember, the seller needs to remain anonymous so that house hunters can project their own lives into your space.

At this point you may be wondering if you need to have a steady hand and perfect writing to pull this off. No problem! There are a number of interior typography companies specializing in providing ultra-thin stick-on words and letters that look like wall writing but are actually removable. If you don't like where your word is placed, move it higher, lower, turn it at an angle, or put it in another room entirely.

One such manufacturer, www.wonderfulgraffiti.com, provides stick-on words and letters in many different colors, fonts and sizes. You get to choose what you want to say, play with the style and size, and even try your words out on a virtual wall on your computer screen to see how they look before you place your order.

Who wouldn't remember walking into a guest bathroom which delivers the message "Mirror, mirror on the wall, who is the fairest of them all?" encircling a large round mirror? That's the power that words can bring to your home.

▪ Light Up Your Life

It's amazing what the right kind of light hitting the right places can do. Think of art galleries, jewelry stores, clothing boutiques, upscale furniture stores, restaurants and many other businesses. Almost all of them use strategic directed lighting to increase the appeal of both their merchandise and their surroundings.

While your house is on the market you are in the business of selling too. So it's important to light your merchandise—meaning your home—in an advantageous way. This is something most home sellers don't think about. They think that as long as the light switches work, all is well. But there's so much more to lighting that you can do. Luckily you can enhance the look of your lights quickly and inexpensively.

First, there's the color of the light itself. You want bulbs that deliver a warm glow or a full spectrum effect, rather than those that emit a cool bluish tinge. These days natural spectrum and fluorescent bulbs that emit a sunny glow are easy to find. Take a look at http://www.realgoods.com to see the types of "indoor sunshine" bulbs that are currently available.

The placement of your lights is also important. A single overhead light isn't the most attractive lighting strategy for a room. It may be functional, but it can make a room look flat and washed out. If you want to light up certain features, such as a painting, a colored wall, an architectural niche, or anything else of interest in a room, it's better to bring in a directed light source. One fast way to do this is to get a track light or "tree lamp" with several bulbs and point them toward the areas you want to illuminate.

Even if your home showings take place during the day, it's a good idea to turn on directed lights to add extra appeal to your rooms. If you walk through a model home, you'll notice that they do this. Clearly, for economic and ecological reasons you don't want to burn your lights all day, but during home showings it's worth turning them on for a short time.

If you've got a room with little natural light and only a gloomy overhead fixture, turn on a lamp or bounce light with a full spectrum bulb during showings to keep people from flipping on the overhead light. By doing this, home buyers get to see your rooms, literally, in the best possible light.

If you have old unattractive light fixtures, you can give your house a quick facelift by swapping them with some new, more attractive ones. They can cost very little, from $15 or so, and can shift the personality of a room to go along with your theme.

I'll never forget when I was a kid, hunting for a new house with my mother, and finding one that had a little glowing lantern above the kitchen counter. My brother and I fell in love with it and lobbied hard for that house—just because of the light fixture! Luckily my mother took into account our opinions when making her final decision. I am happy to report that we ended up buying the house and I spent many happy years turning on and off that little light. Of course that wasn't the only reason my mother decided on this house. It had more to do with the price and school district, but the light fixture did sell us kids on the place!

■ Swap Your Switch Plates

Now here's a simple trick: replace your white plastic switch plates with something more interesting. No one usually thinks about these plates, but when you swap them for something with some color and design, people notice. This is another little change that could make a big difference in how your home is remembered. People can actually develop a crush on your house because of your switch plates.

I saw it happen with my own eyes in one home we had. It was a tract home that looked like every other home in the neighborhood, but I changed the switch plates in each room so they matched the décor. Some of the plates I bought at art fairs and home stores, some I created on my own by applying colorful mosaics and grout right over the original plates, and some I painted over using stencils.

When it came time to sell that house our real estate agent reported that people were constantly remarking on the switch plates because it made our house unique. Not surprisingly, when we found a buyer, one of the conditions for the sale was that the new owner got to keep all of our switch plates. It turned out that this little touch had a big influence on the buyer's decision.

I was a little sad giving up those switch plates, but being they helped seal the deal on the house, I was willing to part with them. Besides, it meant I could go out and buy new ones in our next house.

There are so many ways to change the look of your switch plates these days. You can go to a do-it-yourself pottery store that lets you paint and glaze your own ceramic switch plates, you can apply fabric or wallpaper to them, or you can purchase them from many sources. Do an Internet search on "light switch plates" and you'll find many online stores that carry them, including http://www.switchhits.com and http://www.switchplategallery.com.

■ Change Your Drawer Pulls

Now this may sound frivolous, but your drawer pulls do matter. In fact, some people might walk away after a showing and think a lot about your drawer pulls. Once, a friend who was house hunting called to tell me about a place she had just seen. "It was hideously ugly!" she said. When I asked why, she told me it had horrible drawer pulls. "Every one of them had a big ugly gold flower on it." That is what she remembered most about the entire house!

If drawer pulls can have that kind of negative impact, then it makes sense that the right drawer pulls can have some sort of influence in a more positive direction. And, it turns out that they can.

Earlier, I mentioned how I changed the drawer pulls in my laundry room from plain white ones to blue checkered ones. That little change added a lot of charm to the room. In fact, one of the comments we heard back from would-be buyers was that they really appreciated our drawer pulls. It was just one more thing that gained us a green checkmark.

Try this little exercise right now: imagine a plain white kitchen with plain white cabinets and drawer pulls. Now, imagine exchanging those drawer pulls for bright red ones. Now visualize them as a cheerful checkerboard yellow. See the difference these small changes can make in a room?

Now take a look at the drawer pulls in your house. Can they be replaced with something more attractive or colorful? The little things do matter. A set of beautiful drawer pulls might be the tipping point that makes a buyer decide on your house rather than another!

▪ Mobilize Your Environment

It seems everyone likes mobiles. Hang one from your ceiling and it brings an instant sense of energy, art, whimsy, sophistication, or intellect to a room. Mobiles also add visual variety to break up a large expanse of blank ceiling space. In addition, many Feng Shui experts recommend hanging a mobile in certain areas of your home to break up stagnant energy and add energetic movement and flow to your environment.

What makes mobiles even more appealing is how easy they are to install. Just put a little hook in your ceiling, hang up your mobile in any room—from your kitchen to your study, or even your bathroom or garage, and you're in business. You've got instant sophistication.

The hardest part is choosing a mobile from the multitudes of styles available. Do an online search and you'll see how many companies sell them and how many choices there are. For example, at http://www.hangingmobilegallery.com and http://www.konrads.com, you'll find hundreds of choices: from swirling leaves and abstracts, to hot air balloons and musical notes. There are mobiles to fit every color scheme, room theme, size and price range.

When looking for a mobile, select one with thin metal or invisible plastic wires that brings a sense of elegance to your space. In other words, don't hang up one of the cheap toy store mobiles featuring paper planets hung on tangled pieces of thick string. That would defeat your purpose entirely.

You can pick up an attractive mobile on eBay for under $20 (look under "hanging mobile") or choose from hundreds of styles in the $30–$75 range offered at home decorator shops. The other great thing about mobiles is that even though they help differentiate your house from your competition, when it's time to move out, your mobiles come with you. You don't have to leave them behind like you do your light fixtures, garden and paint job.

▪ Roll Out The Purple Carpet

You can quickly change the feel of a room by laying down an area rug. In just a couple of seconds you can take a dull, non-memorable room and make it cozy, dramatic, warm, or color-ful just by rolling out a carpet.

Area rugs also help break up a large room into a variety of smaller functional areas. For example, put a rug under your dining table and chairs, even if your dining area is part of your living room, and suddenly it feels as if you've got a separate dining room.

Put a rug under your favorite chair, bookcase and lamp and now you've created a separate reading nook. If you put up a dividing screen, it will actually feel as if you've created a new room, without paying thousands to construct walls.

With all the colors, styles and shapes available you can find an area rug to fit any room theme. You can even choose one made of bamboo or wood strips to bring a tropical or Asian feel to your space. Or, choose a bold design to make a plain room suddenly appear modern or wild.

Even if you have wall-to-wall carpet, you can still use area rugs on top of it to add personality or differentiate your room space. (Just remember to put down a thin pad between the area rug and the carpet so the rug colors don't bleed into the carpet. Also, if you keep the rug there for years, the carpet underneath may be a bit darker color due to constant sun exposure everywhere else in the room.)

■ Toss in Some Pillows

One way to make a room look instantly warmer and more welcoming is to add a few big cushy pillows. You don't have to just pile them on a couch or chairs either. Throw some big pillows down on your carpet and you might find some of your friends stretched out across your floor. Not only do pillows lead to relaxation and easy-going informal gatherings, they'll also cost you a lot less than new couches and chairs will.

Pillows actually contribute four things to your room: comfort, style, color and new places to sit. You don't even have to get new pillows if you already have some. If they are old, stained or ripped, just pop your pillows into new fabric covers and you've got instant color and style to compliment the theme of your room.

Pillows also let you go a little wild in the design department. You can mix solid color pillow covers with polka dots, stripes, sequins, paisleys or flowers and no one will scream and call the fashion police. You can even clash pillow colors and keep all your old friends.

■ Add Smoke and Mirrors (But leave out the smoke)

Do you want to make your rooms look more spacious without knocking down walls? Do you want to double an attractive view outside your window? Do you want to increase the brightness of your room without spending extra on lights and electricity? All of this can be accomplished simply by hanging mirrors in strategic locations. Mirrors can create magical illusions in space, making rooms look larger, brighter and better.

I guess that's why the term "smoke and mirrors" refers to creating magical illusions. Add a few mirrors and it can dramatically influence the feel of an entire room. When I purchased my very first piece of real estate, a tiny studio condo in San Francisco, it was a mirror that gave it a million dollar ambiance. Above my fireplace I installed a huge mirror to reflect the floor to ceiling view outside my window.

Even though my studio was only 632 square feet, the mirror made the whole space look expansive and bright. During the day it reflected the entire sky and cityscape, and at night it brought in all of the city lights twinkling from every direction. To enhance the look even more, I bought a glass dining table, coffee table and end tables so that the light would bounce off every surface.

When I visited my neighbors' identical condos, which still had the original wood paneling above their fireplaces instead of a mirror, I was always surprised at how dark and small these condos really were. It was only the mirror and glass surfaces that saved my studio from being another depressing little box. Not only did the mirror dramatically enhance the ambiance of my place, when it was time to sell, my condo sold for more than the other similar units. Ever since then I've been a big fan of mirrors.

You don't have to have an incredible view to be sold on mirrors though. Even a view of the sky will add a sense of space and brightness. And if your mirror has a lovely frame, you'll also add style and elegance. In fact, you don't even need a beautiful frame. Just take a regular mirror and drape some fabric over the edges.

One smart spa owner drapes beautiful scarves over her plain frameless mirrors in her massage rooms to give each room a luxurious touch. Not only do the rooms look beautiful during the day, at night when the spa is closed she wears these scarves out on the town as attractive, wearable art. To me this is the essence of making the most of what you've got!

■ Go for the Highs and Lows

Walk into your average room and you'll be met with a sea of furniture that is of roughly the same height. Most everything in the room falls within a range of 1.5 feet off the ground to around 3 feet off the ground. This includes couches, dining tables, chairs, coffee tables, end tables, beds, nightstands, dressers, chests, and desks. Furniture of this height breaks up a room into two distinct halves: the bottom half, which holds almost all of the furniture, and the top half, which is relatively empty except for a few paintings in most cases.

Rooms like this can bore the eyes. Eyes have much more fun when they can wander around a room and jump from elevation to elevation. By varying the height of your furniture you can break up the uniformity and ordinariness of a room. For example, add a tall bistro table and high-backed chairs next to a series of short, different sized vases. Or, place a tall bookshelf next to an area rug with a few large cushy floor pillows for lounging. Now your eyes can have some fun.

Some other things you can do to add visual variety is to use tall floor lamps, living trees, armoires, candelabras and hanging silk lanterns to give your room height. Then use low Asian tables, short statues, rugs and floor baskets to fill in the lower elevations. You can quickly make a low sitting area by covering a round circle of wood or glass with some attractive fabric and putting a couple of big pillows out for lounging.

For even more visual variety add a couple of surprises to a room. Make an alluring coffee or martini-sipping spot by placing a high bistro table and a couple of tall chairs next to a window in your bedroom. Or, create a clever little reading area in your den by bringing in a woven hammock and a bright red umbrella. Scenes like these not only add elevation, they beckon the viewer to join the fun.

If you can make buyers' eyes scan a room and find it visually fascinating, your home will have a better chance of being remembered.

■ Bring in a Fountain

Fountains do a paradoxical thing: they bring tranquility to a room while they simultaneously uplift and add energy. If you want a quick way to make people feel calmer while also more energized, get a fountain. This is why you often see them in health spas. These fountains can have a positive effect on both your mind and body, and help you rationalize why you might shell out big bucks for a one-hour health spa experience. By adding a fountain or fountains around your home, you can duplicate this same feeling—helping potential buyers rationalize why they should spend money on your home.

Nowadays you can find interesting, inexpensive fountains everywhere, from gift stores to hardware stores. I saw a beautiful little fountain at the drugstore recently for $24. However, make sure to find a fountain that is proportionate to your room size. If you've got a large living room, entry area or kitchen, you'll need to make a bigger splash to get noticed. But for a small bedroom, office, or bathroom, a peaceful little burble is all you need.

■ Get Yourself Some Plant Friends

Something nice happens when rooms are shared with living green things. The room feels more alive and the people inside it feel better without knowing why. That's because plants don't give themselves much credit for what they do. They work 24/7 to remove air pollutants, add oxygen and beautify the room, all without asking for a paycheck.

Plants can also add to the theme of a room. A couple of cactuses will bring a southwest or Mexican touch to a room. Bamboo will compliment an Asian theme, or you can bring in some tropical plants to go along with a beach or an island-themed room. Plants are also great for taking up space and adding life to a room that doesn't have much furniture or personality. Just add a couple of hard-to-kill Peace Lilies and any room will look happier.

The only rule is to keep your plants healthy looking. Droopy dying plants do not earn you green checkmarks. Instead they can earn you the opposite. So make sure to monitor your plants for dying leaves, give them a good dusting, and prop up your droopy plants with a stick so they look happier.

If you've got a plant that looks a little sick no matter how much you baby it, give it to a neighbor with a green thumb. Don't have it out on display when your house is on the market. A sick looking plant can subtly distract from an otherwise lovely room.

To this day, I remember touring a house that had a bright living room with a number of plants hanging from the ceiling.

They might have looked charming, if it weren't for the fact that these plants had long, thin straggly vines that had grown all the way down to the floor and were growing across the carpet. Don't let this happen to you!

If you aren't confident in your plant growing ability, go to a nursery and ask which plants are the hardest to kill. They can fix you up with some new green friends that will work hard for you and ask little in return.

■ Smell Helps Sell

It's widely known that smell is our most primitive, most emotional sense. The right scent can invoke instant feelings of joy, comfort, serenity, even passion. But the wrong smell can make us want to run out of a house in disgust. In this section we'll talk only about the good smells; later when we talk about how to avoid getting red checkmarks, we'll get into stinks.

Most everyone has heard that baking bread or a pan of brownies right before a showing can make a home smell very inviting. This is indeed a good idea. Your house will smell great and if nothing comes out of the showing, at least you'll have something yummy to eat.

The beauty of this technique is that even if people know they are being manipulated by a wonderful smell, it still works. That's why some movie theatres pump the smell of popcorn out onto the sidewalk, and cookie shops aim their oven vents directly on pedestrians as they pass by. The right aroma is hard to resist.

My friend Barbara, who is well versed in the power of smell, used this technique with wonderful results. When she found out that a British couple was interested in her house and coming to see it again, she quickly cooked up a batch of buttery scones. The couple didn't mind that the owner was home, and in fact were delighted when my friend invited them to sit down and enjoy fresh hot scones and tea. Sitting in Barbara's aromatic kitchen, the couple decided they felt so happy and at home there, that they would buy the place. To this day my friend attributes the sale of her house to the power of smell.

But wait, you say you're on a diet? Or you don't have time to bake before a home showing? No problem. You can still seduce someone using scent sticks. If you've never run across them before, I'll tell you how they work: scent sticks are long thin reeds that are dipped in a bottle of essential oil or another fragrance. The oil evaporates slowly through the sticks, releasing and diffusing whatever wonderful smell was in the bottle.

There are dozens and dozens of scents to choose from that go along with the theme or function of your rooms. For example, you can have your bedroom hint of lavender, your study smelling like fine leather, and your kitchen smelling like fresh baked bread or cinnamon.

Normally I'm not a big fan of artificial chemical smells, but this is the exception. Good quality scent sticks really can make a room more inviting, and might just put a house hunter in a buying mood.

▪ Watch Your Windows

If eyes are the windows to the soul, then what are windows? Windows are actually the eyes in your room, illuminating everything around you. And to continue this metaphor, curtains and rods are like eyelashes and eyeliner that frame the eyes and draw attention to them. But unlike human eyes, even if the windows are closed and the drapes are drawn, they can still communicate a lot about a room.

To make your windows look their best, keep them sparkling clean and frame them with attractive curtains and curtain rods. If you've got old dingy window coverings, give them a good washing or get some new ones. It's amazing how sophisticated or cheerful a room can become just by changing your curtains.

And curtains don't have to be curtains either: they can be scarves, swags, roll ups, shutters, blinds, sewn sheets, or even a nice pair of cotton shower curtains! One of the nicest window treatments I've ever seen was simply a Japanese obi belt from a kimono, zigzagged across a decorative curtain rod. The colors in the obi picked up the colors in both the furniture and the rug, bringing the whole room together.

In rooms with a great view where privacy isn't an issue, a scarf, swag or obi is all you need to make a window look dressed up, without covering it up. In rooms where there is a great view, but you also want some privacy, you have two interesting options: one is to get "top down" window shades that let you open the shade as little or as much as you want, starting from the top of your windows, going down. (Warning: these can be expensive.) The other option is to install a tension rod and curtains across your window frame so that the bottom half of the window is covered, but the top half is exposed. (This is the cheaper way to go.) Either of these options will give you privacy while simultaneously letting you look out your window and enjoy the view.

I once stayed at a bed and breakfast that was surrounded by huge oak trees, where the owner had hung lacy curtains on tension rods across the bottom half of all the windows. This gave all the guests a sense of privacy from the street, but still afforded a view of the magnificent trees while lying in bed.

When framing your windows, you should also take a look at your curtain rods. Are they the old plastic drab ones that no one ever notices? If so, you might consider changing them too. Go to Walmart, PriceMart, Target, or maybe even your neighborhood hardware store and you'll find all sorts of creative, yet inexpensive rods and finials. (Finials are the caps at the end of your curtain rods that keep the curtains from slipping off while adding even more personality to your window treatment.)

These days, rods and finials have become works of art, resembling tree branches, kings' staffs, tridents, golden pineapples, crystal balls, and many other styles. Or, if you want to go natural, make your own rods from real tree branches or bamboo poles.

If you've got a beautiful view out your window, you've got the best of both worlds. You can open your drapes and let the world pour in, while still creating a beautiful frame through the use of curtains, rods and finials. If your view is not very appealing, just keep the curtains closed and make your window treatments or what's in front of them grab the spotlight.

■ Feng Shui Your Home

No conversation about changing the feeling of your environment would be complete without mentioning Feng Shui, the ancient Chinese art of enhancing the flow of energy in your home by moving your laundry basket out of the living room.

Feng Shui is all about changing the placement of items in your rooms, reducing clutter, and putting objects such as fountains, chimes, mobiles, house plants, and mirrors in strategic places in your home to shift and increase the flow of energy.

When done correctly, Feng Shui can make your home feel more alive—which can also make it more sellable. There are two ways to go about getting "Feng Shuid." The first is to hire someone who does it for a living, who can quickly step in and point out what you need to move, remove or add. These experts often point out things you may not have even noticed, such as a chair with a broken seat in your backyard that needs to be fixed or removed because it's causing energy stagnation outside your door. (This is a true example.)

If you prefer not to hire your own Feng Shui expert, you can purchase a book and make some changes yourself. There are dozens of good manuals on the subject that will help you inspect your environment for energy blocks room by room, and make positive, attractive changes. This method, of course, will be a lot cheaper than hiring an expert, but it's hard to see your house in the same light as an expert who has a trained Feng Shui eye. However, even making small changes, such as removing the laundry basket can make a big difference to the feel of a room.

Not only will a dose of Feng Shui enhance the flow of energy through your home, followers of Feng Shui firmly believe that it can also positively affect your health, well-being, prosperity, and relationships. If you can get all of this by making a few simple adjustments to your environment, it might be worth giving it a try.

Even if you're not a believer in the "energy" aspects of Feng Shui, this practice still consists of good design principles that can help you attractively organize your environment.

■ Make Your Home Feel Loved

There is a sad real estate term that refers to houses that have been on the market for an extended period of time without selling. The term is called "stale" and you can often feel it when you walk into a house that has been on the market too long. The owners have stopped primping and pampering it for showings and they've fallen out of love with it.

You can see subtle signs of a stale house everywhere . . . dust accumulating in the corners and along window ledges, newspapers and magazines piling up on countertops, and dead leaves collecting on the side of the house. You can tell the owners have been losing hope and they've been blaming their house for messing up their lives.

If this sounds familiar, you need to start loving your home again—even if you dearly want to leave it. You've got to treat it special. Buy it flowers. Bake it cookies that fill the rooms with the comforting scent of caring. Get rid of the piles of paper and make your surface areas shine again.

If you treat your house with respect and love, your buyers will feel it. It's a lot like people who take good care of themselves—others are more inclined to take an interest in them too.

■ Remember What First Attracted You

Do you remember what first attracted you to your home? Was it the view out your windows? The sparkling expanses of tile? Whatever it was, make sure those qualities still stand out because the next buyer may be attracted to the same things you were.

It's easy to take your home's attractive features for granted to the point that you don't even notice them anymore. One couple I know was originally attracted to their house because they fell in love with the mountain views outside their kitchen window. They imagined themselves standing at the sink and enjoying the vista while doing their dishes. But over time the trees outside the house had grown to the point where they had almost completely obstructed the scenery. Rather than a dramatic view, they now had a pleasant view of rustling leaves.

Wisely, they hired an arborist to trim their trees to the point where they could see their mountains again. Sure enough, they noticed that people coming to their open houses remarked, "Imagine looking out of your window at that view while washing the dishes!" In the end, that great view helped sell the house again.

Now, take a look at your home. Are the original qualities that attracted you still present? Just like an old sweetheart, don't forget what drew you together. That's how you can help draw in your home's next lover.

▪ Make a Portrait of Your Home

There is something about having a portrait or an attractive photo of your house on display to make it look more charming and special. It's similar to royalty and the ultra wealthy who commission artists to paint their portraits and then hang them in gilded frames on their walls. Just the act of painting a subject or object in question makes it seem more worthy and significant.

I know you might be thinking, "I live in a little house, who needs a picture of that?" Believe it or not, it works for even small tract houses. Just the fact that you view your house as important enough to warrant artwork created from it shows that it's loved and respected. And if one person shows that they've clearly loved your home, it will be easier for the next person to see it as loveable.

It's like the ugly ex-boyfriend phenomenon. Even if he's ugly, the fact that he had a previous girlfriend when he goes back on the market makes him more interesting to the next candidates. If he'd always been single, others might question his lovability and see him as less wanted.

So consider creating an image of your home, either by taking an artful photo or having someone draw it, paint it, or do a pastel or charcoal sketch of it. If you are artistic, this can be a fun assignment. If you aren't, you can find someone at your local college or high school to create an image for you.

Next, pick a mood or time of day to best capture your home. It can be on a rainy, moody day, or during a gorgeous sunset, in the midst of spring flowers, or lit up on a dark night. Then have the picture signed by the artist for further proof of its importance. For a final touch, put it on an easel or place it in a beautiful frame for all to see.

Not only will this image attest to how much you treasure your home, you can also use it as a marketing tool. Make your image into a postcard or incorporate it into your home's marketing website to make it stand out from the rest. How many other homes do you see with portraits painted of them? This is a great way to attract curiosity and gain further attention.

CHAPTER FIVE

How To Eliminate Red Checkmarks Inside Your Home

Now that we've covered what you can do inside your house to get more green checkmarks, let's talk about how to avoid getting the red ones. Because you live in your home and see it every day, it can be difficult to look at it from the standpoint of an outsider. Therefore, it's a good idea to have a close, but brutally honest friend take a walk through your property and point out things that might work against you.

If you don't have the stomach to ask someone else to do this, you may be able to do it yourself. But, you'll need to pretend you're a picky stranger seeing your place for the first time. This can be difficult, but not impossible. However, you'll need to be totally honest and write down a list of all the things you find that need fixing and changing.

Here is a list of items that can earn you dreaded red checkmarks. Knock them off one at a time and you'll increase the chance of finding a buyer for your home.

■ Cut the Clutter

Eliminating clutter can't be overstated. If your place is loaded with stuff, people won't see your home, they'll mainly see your stuff—which can earn you a big red checkmark. (Especially if there are other comparable houses on the market that are cleaner.)

Not only does clutter make it difficult for house hunters to imagine fitting their own belongings into your house, they'll also wonder whether you're hiding something behind all those things. They may wonder, "Are the walls moldy behind those boxes? Is the rug stained beneath those stacks of magazines? Is that pile of laundry hiding a gaping hole in your floor?"

The more open space you show, the more people are able to mentally inspect your home for defects. If they see clean walls, floors, closets and countertops, they'll know what they are actually buying.

The challenge is that if you've been in a house for more than several years, clutter slowly creeps up on you. You might start with just a few cherished items on your kitchen counter-top, but then someone buys you a nice vase, so you put that on display. Then you buy a great set of knives and a wooden chopping block. No problem. Then you add a couple of cook-books . . . and then a couple more. You get the picture. Before you know it, the whole countertop is covered. But it happened so slowly you didn't notice the change. Unfortunately, the exact people you need to impress will instantly notice the clutter and be turned off by it all.

So if you really want to avoid this red checkmark, cut your clutter by at least half. It may feel like a shock to the system, but once you've done it, you'll notice that it feels good and your rooms will look more spacious.

▪ Rent a Storage Space

Now that I've suggested that you take half of all of your belongings away, I can hear you asking, "So where am I going to put all my stuff? If I can't just move it to another room because then I'll clutter up that space and I don't want to give it away, what do I do with it all?"

The best answer is to rent a temporary storage closet (if you can afford to do this), until your property sells. If you rent one close by, you can almost consider it an extension of your home where you can go and visit your stuff whenever you like. The funny thing is, most people who rent storage space notice that they seldom need the items they put in it. That's because we can actually get by with much less than we think.

Storage closets are great places to put all of your holiday decorations, half-finished craft projects, boxes of photos, luggage, car parts, gardening equipment that you don't need for part of the year, and all those things you just can't bear to give away yet.

Of course it would be better to not need to pay rent for a storage space, but it could be the lesser of two evils if clutter is making it difficult to sell your house. If at all possible, try to narrow down what you really need to keep so you can rent a smaller, cheaper storage space.

If you are worried about theft, select a facility with a manager who lives on site. If possible, try to find a unit that the manager can actually see from his or her living space. You can also take out an insurance policy to cover your belongings, however these policies do not usually cover large amounts. So it's best that you don't put your ancient, treasured vases from the Ming Dynasty in there. But your grandma's old chair and spare car parts? Perfect.

■ Fix What's Broken

You may hardly notice the broken things around your house because you can get used to living with them. However, a house hunter will notice these, even if only on a subconscious level. They notice loose doorknobs, chipped tile, squeaky cabinet doors, cracked toilet seats, dripping faucets, lights that don't turn on, and peeling caulk around the tub. What makes it worse is they don't forget these images. It's similar to meeting a salesman for the first time and noticing a stain on his shirt. You might immediately judge his character as sloppy, and it can affect how you relate to him.

That's why it's important to search out and fix anything broken. If everything is well functioning, it's easier to give buyers the impression that your home is almost maintenance-free. They won't need to come armed with a crew of repair people before they move into your place, and they won't need a bunch of tools to keep it that way.

Some house hunters may actually be interested in a house with a lot of flaws because they think they can offer you a rock-bottom "as-is" price. But if you want to sell your home for the highest amount possible, get it fixed up before you put it on the market.

▪ Get the Stains Out

You also may not notice stains slowly creeping into your life. Sometimes it happens so sneakily you might think they were there all along, so you need to conduct a thorough stain check.

Is the grout between your kitchen or bathroom tiles discolored? If so, scrub it with a toothbrush and a good cleanser. If you can't restore it to its original color, use a grout pen to retouch it. These pens let you simply draw a line over the stained grout to bring it back to life. This is actually pretty fun because you receive immediate gratification as you draw each line.

How about your walls, bathtubs, sinks and faucets? Some heavy-duty scrubbing may be in order. But, remember this is also good exercise. You may be able to substitute this for a day at the gym.

Give all of your rugs a good carpet cleaning. Over time they can dramatically lose their perkiness and look old and tired. This alone can make a big difference in the freshness of your place. The same goes for your curtains. An accumulation of dust can make them look dull and shabby. Throw them in the wash, or get them dry-cleaned.

Do not ignore these pesky little tasks and think no one will notice. Everything in your house is subconsciously judged for cleanliness and newness. For some inexplicable reason, people just don't like other people's old dirt.

■ Clean Your Edges and Corners

A nifty place for dust and dirt to hang out is along all the ledges, edges and corners of your walls and windows. Even if you've never dropped or spilled anything, the dirt mysteriously comes. So you need to be especially vigilant of these areas.

One of the best tools for getting rid of this dirt is with a Shop Vac. These industrial-strength vacuums can suck up every last molecule of dirt in their path. In fact, there is almost nothing that gives me greater pleasure than running my Shop Vac nozzle along my ledges and edges and seeing them come clean instantly.

If you don't own one of these handy vacuums, find a friend who does and ask to borrow it in exchange for a batch of brownies. You'll both be happy. And remember, there's a lot of cleanliness right underneath that dirt!

▪ Keep Your Kitchen Cupboards Clean

Even though you think your food is hidden safely behind closed doors and no one will see the syrup stains, spilled sugar, and wayward cereal flakes sitting on the shelves, it will no longer be your secret when your house is on the market.

Whether you like it or not, under the guise of needing to see how much cupboard space you have, house hunters may take a look around. But if they see a mess, you're open to receiving red checkmarks.

That's why it's important to organize your food cupboards and keep your shelves clean and attractive. Not everyone will look of course, but all it takes is the one person who is getting serious about your home to see dirty cupboard shelves and interpret it as a character flaw of your house.

So don't give buyers anything they can use against you—even if it's behind closed doors. Shop Vacs, by the way, do a great job of cleaning dirty cupboards, and no, I do not own any stock in the Shop Vac company.

▪ Keep Your Windows, Glass and Mirrors Clean

Before I go into a new restaurant, I always notice how clean the restaurant staff keep their windows and front door, especially if the door is glass. This is a tip-off that can tell me a lot about the cleanliness of the entire place. If the first thing I see is fingerprints and dirty glass, I can imagine what I might find in the restaurant's private kitchen.

This also applies to the windows in your home. If the first thing home buyers see is streaked, dusty, or finger-printed windows, they might make an immediate judgment about the care you take of your home. And like all first impressions, they can be hard to undo.

So make it a point to keep your windows clean—in particular, those that people see first when they walk up to your front door. If your house has been on the market for an extended period, remember to clean them on a regular basis. They may have been spotless and sparkling when you first put your house up for sale, but over time they can get mighty dirty. This same thing goes for your glass shower doors and mirrors. Clean glass makes your whole place shine.

■ Get a Giraffe's View

A lot of what you see depends on your height. One time I had a close friend house-sit while I was out of town and my house was on the market. Upon my return she told me that my place could use a good cleaning. I was surprised because I thought I had been taking excellent care of my home.

But the problem was that my house sitter was 6'3" and I'm nearly a foot shorter than her. She had a giraffe's view over my domain and could look down on the top of my canopy bed, stove hood, tall bookshelves, and even the window frames above most of the windows. For me, I had no idea dirt was up there because my worldview stopped around 5'7", which I could only reach on tiptoes or in high heels.

After she left, I stood on a tall chair and did some exploring. My house sitter was right: my range hood was filthy and on top of the poles that framed my canopy bed there was an ugly line of dust half an inch thick. It was an enlightening moment to view the house from her perspective and realize that all the taller people who had been touring my house had a bird's eye view of my high-elevation dirt.

I suppose this works the other way around too. Tall people might not notice accumulations of dust in lower places. So the moral of the story is, whether you're short or tall, be aware that house hunters may be eying your place from a different vantage point, and consider this when cleaning.

■ Don't Put Trashcans on Display

Scientific studies have revealed that most people do not want to view the items contained within other people's trashcans. In fact, even the decorative little containers you see in bathrooms are not that appealing, especially if they contain anything at all. Garbage breaks the mood and illusion of the perfect home. In a fantasy house, people wouldn't generate garbage.

Therefore, the best thing to do with garbage in your kitchen, bath, or any other room is to find a place to hide it. If you've got a cabinet under your sink, that's the perfect place—even if it means buying a shorter can and moving some of the items under your sink somewhere else.

In your home office, hide the trashcan deep under your desk. If you have a trash container in your bedroom consider getting rid of it. If you absolutely, positively have no place to hide your containers and you dearly need them, at least make sure they are empty and there isn't any gunk on the sides of them. If you have no place to hide your kitchen trashcan, get one with a lid and keep it closed. I think the metal ones with a foot pedal are the lesser of all evils.

In addition, if you've got recycle bins hanging out in your house, move them to your garage. As good as it is to recycle, recyclables aren't that attractive either. If you don't have an area outside your home to keep your recycle pile, keep it out of view in a lower drawer, under your kitchen sink, or in a decorative container or a box with a lid.

■ Hide the Ugly Stuff

Sometimes you've got things you just can't put away, such as exposed pipes, a tangle of power cords, or unattractive machinery. If you can't put them away, you can find a way to creatively camouflage them.

One homeowner I worked with had a computer, printer and several hard drives on a desk with a tangle of power cords hanging underneath it. Because it faced the doorway, it was the first thing you saw when you walked in the room, and boy, was that pile of cords ever ugly! So I helped him find a bookcase that was just high enough to hide the cords, which worked perfectly. Not only did it hide the cords, he now had a place to display his most attractive books and rock collection.

Using fabric, folding screens, furniture, fountains and plants, you can actually turn what could have earned you a red checkmark into a green checkmark. You've probably seen this in some restaurants with high ceilings and industrial pipes. Instead of looking like an eyesore, creative owners work around these features by hanging billowing bolts of fabric across the ceiling to create a caravan tent effect. Or, some of them incorporate the pipes into an ultra-modern industrial look, and then charge you an extra $10 per dinner entrée for the experience!

■ Hide the Quirky Stuff

Even though you might enjoy a giant buffalo head hanging over your easy chair, the person looking at your house might not, and you'll get a big red checkmark.

One time I was walking through a Sunday open house, along with a number of other people, and in one of the bedrooms there was a huge car hood from a 1950's truck chained and bolted to the wall. I watched as visitor after visitor walked into that room and exclaimed, "Eewww!" and then walked out of that house for good. All it took was one old car hood.

That "creative touch" was probably from some well-loved vehicle that the owner cherished. But for everyone else it was an eyesore that they'd remember above anything else. That's why it's important to remove things that scream out, "This house belongs to someone who isn't at all like me." Remember, all of the little (and big) things count.

■ Get Rid of the Smelly Stuff

Here's something you shouldn't do before a home showing: cook up a bunch of hard boiled eggs, steam up a head of cauliflower, or have a fish fry. When house hunters enter your place, you'll immediately get a red checkmark for housing a nasty smell. People have a hard time seeing beyond the smell, even if they are in the midst of a sparkling clean, attractive home.

Some other aromas to watch out for might smell good *to you*, like the smell of curry, but to others it may smell frightfully exotic. Some buyers won't be able to imagine themselves living in a place that has harbored such a foreign smell.

Another cooking aroma you may need to be aware of is the smell of cooked or grilled meat. In areas where there are high numbers of vegetarians, you might turn off a potential buyer simply by grilling up a batch of hamburgers before a showing.

A strict vegetarian I know told me she would never consider buying a house if she walked in and smelled cooked meat. Even though she knew that if she bought the place that smell would go away, she'd always remember that meat was once cooked in there. Therefore, you should definitely consider your timing before cooking up anything with a lasting meaty smell, especially if you live in a city with a high veggie population, such as Portland, San Francisco, or Berkeley.

This isn't to say you can never cook up your favorite fragrant foods while your house is on the market, you just need to pay attention to possible home showings and use fans or open windows liberally. Or, wait until the showing is over before frying up some bacon.

It's not just cooking odors you have to think about either. Check to make sure there aren't any old food smells coming from your garbage cans, disposal or refrigerator. Also, make sure there are no mystery smells emanating from other rooms in your home.

For example, does your rug have a slightly mildewy smell? Do you have an aromatic pooch or stinky cat litter box? Does your house smell of old cigarette smoke that has permeated the walls, curtains and furniture? These smells, if bad enough, can turn a buyer off to the point where they won't even consider your house.

The challenge is that as the inhabitant of your home, you might not notice certain smells exist because they creep up slowly. I once attended a surprise party hosted by a woman I didn't know very well. When I walked into her front door for the first time there was a horrible, unexplainable smell that greeted me. But I doubt that she was aware of it because it had probably been there for quite some time. Even her closest friends may not have mentioned it to her because there was no good way of saying, "Gee, your house smells horrible!"

If you've got a brutally honest friend or two and you suspect that your home may harbor a stink, ask them to be honest with you. Their honesty just might help you sell your house.

In terms of getting rid of the bad smells, keep your refrigerator and cabinets as clean as possible, make sure the sink disposal isn't trapping old food, take the garbage out every twenty minutes, sanitize the dog, steam clean your carpets and furniture if necessary, and repaint your walls if they house long-established smoking fumes.

■ Use Your Rooms Right

Okay, let's say you don't need your dining room, so you turn it into an office space. That might work well for you, but if you keep it looking like an office when your house is on the market, you're going to confuse some buyers. They won't be able to visualize your house having a dining room, even though the room clearly looks like a space where a dining room could be.

You are much better off reverting your rooms back to their original purpose before you try selling your house, or you might just earn yourself a red checkmark for confusing a potentially unimaginative buyer. This goes for any room you're using for an unexpected purpose. Even if you're using a bedroom as an office, you might consider adding a futon or day bed to the room just to give buyers the signal that yes, indeed, this room can easily be used as a bedroom.

■ Figure In Furniture

As bad as clutter is, so can be a starkly empty house. Vacant homes can feel cold and abandoned, and if there are other similar vacant homes on the market, it will be harder for your house to compete. After all, you are offering the same exact thing as others. By adding or keeping some furniture in your home, it will feel friendlier. In fact, if you put furniture into a vacant house you actually have a little advantage over people who live in their home while it's on the market, because you don't have the typical dirt and clutter that accumulates in a "lived-in" house.

And there's another reason why it's a good idea to have some furniture in your rooms: many bedrooms, for example, look microscopically small without furniture in them. You can't imagine the room holding anything more than a little bed. But when it's furnished you might be surprised to see that it can fit a double bed, a dresser and a night table, with room to spare.

People also have a hard time mentally arranging where furniture should go if a room is empty. They often think that furniture should only go against the walls. But when house hunters see a place creatively furnished, they realize they have other choices. If they see that you've placed your couch in the middle of the room, or at a slant, or by the window they can better see the potential for their own things.

But where do you get this furniture if you've already shipped your furniture to another location? One of the best ideas I've heard is to offer to borrow your friends' surplus furniture, which they may be keeping in a paid storage closets or cramming into their own garages. This can be a two-way blessing. You get free furniture, and they get a free place to store their stuff.

Also, check out local garage sales. A lot of times people are willing to part with their furniture for very low prices. Toward the end of a garage sale people are willing to give you even more incredible deals just so you'll haul their unsold items away. This can be a great way to cheaply pick up chairs, desks, tables, lamps and other accessories.

I can attest to this myself. During the final hours of our garage sale a man came by with a truck and offered to take all of our unsold possessions off our hands. This was actually a blessing because we didn't have any more time to figure out how to sell or give it away, and we would've had to hire a hauler to do it for us. So we gave this man a big pile of old furniture and we all won. If you're at the right place at the right time, you may score well by visiting garage sales.

While you are at it, keep an eye out for inexpensive (or free) accessories. A room with just a couch and a table can look pretty lonely. Try adding a painting here, a couple of books there, and a plant in the corner. Suddenly the room will come alive, making it easier for house hunters to establish an emotional connection to your place.

■ Get Your Home Inspected

Do you really know what is going on inside and outside your house? Many sellers are unaware of the problems until an interested buyer hires a home inspector. That's when owners often discover hidden flaws that squeamish buyers can use as rightful opportunities to make demands or walk away from the deal.

To keep this from happening, it's a wise idea to hire your own licensed home inspector *before* you put your house on the market. The inspector can tell you what the issues are in your home, so you can remedy them before they are discovered during a potential home sale.

By dealing with the problems in advance, you eliminate the stress and possible higher cost of trying to make repairs under contract deadlines—or take the risk that the buyer will try to renegotiate the price or walk away from the deal. This is one of the best ways I know of ensuring you won't end up with a big red checkmark against your house at the most crucial time in the sales process.

CHAPTER SIX

How to Increase Green Checkmarks Outside Your Door

You have about two or three seconds to impress a stranger when they are standing outside your home for the first time. As they pull up in front of your property they are internally calculating and asking themselves, "Can I see myself coming home to this place every day? Could I be happy here? Will this place impress others?"

If the answer to any of these questions is "no," your house will earn a big red checkmark, which can be hard to undo no matter what the interior looks like. In fact, a sad-looking exterior can work against you to the point where a buyer may decide to skip your property entirely and move on to the next one.

By making some important little changes to your home's curb appeal, you can turn a buyer's first-impression around. Luckily this doesn't have to translate into a big remodeling job. You can make a number of small exterior changes yourself without having to hire outside help or bring in heavy machinery. The goal is to make your potential buyers feel in the first few seconds that your home is cared for with pride.

Depending upon the style of your house and its location,

you'll find that a number of the following simple touches will apply to your particular property. Even if you live in a condo with an internal hallway, you may still be able to add some small touches that will make your property unique and appealing from the outside.

Here's How:

■ Create a Threshold

Every property, whether it's a villa, cottage or condo, has a line that you cross where you consider yourself home. This is the spot where your personal sanctuary begins—where you can relax, take a deep breath, and drop your street face. In Bali, the threshold of your property is considered sacred, so it's highly recognized and decorated.

If you own a home with a front yard, you may place your threshold next to the street, at the beginning of your walkway, or close to your front porch. If you've got a condo with a front door in an interior hallway, your threshold will be at your door.

But no matter where it begins, you can create a pleasant, symbolic threshold for your home. It can be as simple as an attractive doormat, some special stepping-stones or a few pots of flowers or vases on either side of the path leading to your door. Your threshold can also be a gate, two painted posts, a pair of matching statues, or a wood or metal trellis arch draped with vines or flowers. If you don't have a green thumb, you can just put up an arch and leave it as is—it still makes a great threshold.

Installing a trellis isn't a big operation. Many nurseries sell simple metal ones ready to go, or you can make one of your own. Throughout Latin America, many little homes have a trellis made only of a long thin metal rod, bent into an arch and then covered with flowering vines. This is a spectacularly simple and inexpensive way to say "home sweet home."

Whether house hunters realize it or not, they will fall under the spell of thresholds. Create one that fits your particular environment and you can dramatically increase your home's curb appeal.

▪ Paint Your House a Beautiful Color

One of the greatest lessons I've learned so far involved repainting my house. At the time we were living in a new housing development where all of the homes, block after block, were painted either builder beige, grey, or beige-grey. The only difference was that some houses had three pillars on the front porch and some had four. That's how we could tell them apart.

Right before we put our house up for sale, we decided to paint it a bright, happy farmhouse yellow. When the painting was done I gasped. Our house stood out like a canary on a telephone wire surrounded by grey sparrows. I thought we had made a big mistake. Who would want to buy a house that stuck out like that? I figured we had just limited our potential buyers to a handful of very brave souls.

My feelings were confirmed when I went to a neighborhood party and met a woman who lived several blocks away. She asked me where I lived, and when I asked her if she knew where the bright yellow house was, she squawked, "You don't live next door to *that*, do you?" Then she went on to tell me what an eyesore the house was now.

When I told her that I was the one who painted that house

yellow, she quickly made her escape so she could talk to some regular people. Now I was even more nervous knowing our house was going on the market that very week and there was no way we could repaint it that quickly. (Not to mention the added expense it would cost us.) To make it worse, there were already several other "regular" houses on the market that weren't screaming yellow. So ours, I figured, was a lost cause.

Two days after the house went on the market we received a full price offer. When we met the new buyers, they told us almost sheepishly, that the reason they had picked our place was because they had fallen in love with the paint job. The woman of the house told me she had always dreamed of living in a cute farmhouse-yellow home.

About a year later we drove through our old neighborhood and we were shocked. Almost every house in that area was now painted a bold, bright color. There were beautiful red houses, deep blue ones, sage green ones, and many bright happy yellow ones that looked just like ours.

The entire neighborhood looked like a screaming pack of tropical birds and the area looked terrific. We had started something by being the first to go wild, and then everyone got into the act.

Now of course, not every house will look good painted a bold color. It's much harder to get away with that if you have a southwest pueblo style house or a Georgian-style mansion, but for many houses a few cans of paint can make a beautiful difference.

▪ Add Accent Colors

Maybe you don't want to paint your whole house a bold color. Perhaps you've got the kind of house that looks best in neutral colors, or you don't want to deal with the expense and work of repainting your whole house.

Not to worry! There is something else you can do that will help your house stand out: paint only the trim on your home a second color, such as your railings, gate, shutters, window frames, trellis or just your door. This way you can get a boost of color, but you can accomplish it quickly and easily.

If you plan on painting your whole house a bold color, you can do both: paint your home one color and paint your trim a complementary color. For example, a yellow house can look great with blue trim. (It will make it look like a Swedish storybook cottage.)

Pumpkin color houses also look great with deep blue trim. Southwest style homes stand out with a touch of turquoise or deep purple against a beige color background. Brick red or blue houses look great with white accents. Or, take a white house and paint your door, shutters, and railings black, red, blue, or yellow.

You can get as creative as you want with colors by mixing and matching paint swatches at your local paint store. Or, look at a book that features San Francisco Victorian homes. These places are masterpieces of color, often displaying two or three different complimentary accent colors on the same house.

Depending upon the style of your home, you can add shutters or a gate or a trellis if your home doesn't have these trimmings already. You can then paint them up with an accent color that fits your home's present color. This alone can give your home a tremendous boost.

I've seen dull, square boxes come alive by doing only this. One day on a stroll around my neighborhood, I saw a new home pop up overnight. Then I realized it was a place that had always been there, but the owners had installed window shutters and a trellis painted a bold second color. Suddenly the house was adorable. Before that I had never noticed the place.

■ Get Rid of Roadblocks

One of the important principles in Feng Shui is to minimize the obstacles that block the flow of energy coming into your front door. These obstacles have been cited as causing everything from a lack of money flowing into your life, to a failure to find a spouse.

If at all possible, move items such as big bushes, pots of flowers, and boulders out of the direct path to your door. Understandably, if you have a large tree or a ten-ton boulder you might not be able to do much about it. (Except for changing the actual entry point of your home!) But it can't hurt to examine the pathway leading up your entryway for anything that can be cleared away.

I've heard enough successful Feng Shui stories about people clearing their front paths to make me think it's a worthwhile effort to do so—especially if you're trying to draw people to your front door during a difficult housing market.

■ Give Your House a Name

House naming is an old British custom that started when aristocrats began naming their manors and castles. This custom gradually spread throughout the British Isles to those who owned smaller properties. By naming their homes, owners were able to make a unique and endearing statement about their surroundings.

Nowadays people don't usually think to do this, which is a shame because naming your home is such an easy thing to do and it instantly imparts a sense of charm and personality to your home. People are much more likely to name their boats, RVs, or cabins in recreational areas, but why not give your primary house a name?

I think one of the reasons is that people just don't take the time to think about it, or they are too embarrassed to have the only house around with a name. Or, maybe it's because they think their house looks similar to others, so why treat it special?

Whatever the reason, home naming is something you can do to make your property instantly unique, especially if no one else is doing it! Use this fact to your benefit.

It doesn't matter if your house is a 1950's rancher, a little house in the city, or if it's a tract house in the suburbs, you can still name your home. Just choose a name you like and put it on a sign on your porch or above your front door. I've seen little neighborhoods in the United States where almost every house has a name, and it makes the entire neighborhood more personable.

By home naming of course, I don't mean calling it Fred or Mr. Clark. I'm talking about giving it a lyrical name that captures your home's environment or architecture. Some of the names I've run across include Doves Rest, Hill House, Serenity, The Nook, City Lights, The Oaks, Cozy Corner, Two Gables and Butterfly House.

If you don't have something unusual about your property that inspires a name, you can create one: plant some red roses in your front yard and call your home "The Red Rose." Hang a hammock on your front porch and name your place "The Haven." Or put up a few hummingbird feeders, attract some birds, and get a sign saying "Hummingbird House." See how easy it is to make your home nameable?

Once you've figured out the name, decide on a little plaque or sign that would fit your surroundings and architecture. For example, Mexican and Mediterranean style homes look great with ceramic tile signs. Modern houses look sharp with metal, stone or etched glass signs. Or, if you've got a clapboard farmhouse or shingled bungalow, you might want to choose a wooden sign or even a thin slice from a log.

If you'd like some help, you can hire a sign maker to create your sign for you. You can find these artists locally or look online for someone who specializes in creating signs made out of stone, wood, ceramics or other materials.

For an extra touch, add a little design to your sign, such as flowers, tree branches, or birds to go along with your home's name and theme. For example, if you call your home Casa del Sol (House of the Sun), add a few sun rays to it.

Now just imagine house hunters walking up to your porch and realizing they have discovered a unique sanctuary with its very own name. Another green checkmark will be yours!

■ Show Off Your Numbers

Even the numbers in your street address can be used to add uniqueness and charm to your property. Rather than just having your address stenciled on the mailbox or painted on the curb, you can do much more. Depending upon the style of your home and its environment, here's what you can do:

- Hang up an attractive ceramic plaque with colorful house numbers and flowers painted on it.
- Buy individual wooden number blocks from a hardware

store, paint them a rich color that complements your house, and put them above your garage or in front of your home. For a touch of class, spray-paint the numbers gold, copper or silver, or purchase metal or ceramic decorated numbers.

- Order a wrought iron or metal plaque through an online supplier such as http://www.addressplaqueshops.com. These plaques showcase your address in embossed gold or copper letters, quietly screaming elegance.

- Put a large stone in your front yard with ceramic or metal numbers glued or attached to it, then surround the stone with plants or colorful pots.

Whichever material you use, creating a decorative address is a very easy enhancement to make, and when you combine it with other unique touches, you can dramatically increase the curb appeal of your home.

■ Milk Your Mailbox

If you are lucky enough to have your own mailbox then you have another way to increase the curb appeal of your home. Rather than keeping your mailbox its original black, grey or white, you can get inventive.

One artistic woman repainted her faded black mailbox with big bright orange poppies which she also had all over her garden. This little change made her mailbox an instant area landmark. When neighbors gave out directions to their homes, they'd describe themselves as living one, two or three houses down from the orange poppy mailbox. Just a couple ounces of paint made this woman's home into the focal point of her street!

There are a lot of tastefully decorative things you can do to a mailbox. You can paint it a complementary color that matches your home or trim color, you can add stenciled patterns or flowers using a second color, or you can cover your mailbox with a decorative magnetic mailbox cover, which you can purchase through suppliers such as http://www.curbdecor. com. And, of course, you can purchase a fancy new mailbox at a home supply store, garden shop or over the Internet. Take a look at some of the websites that feature unusual mailboxes, such as http://www.i-mailboxes.com/ and http://www. mailboxworks.com for ideas.

Your mailbox is an extension of your home, so it's important to keep it in good shape. If it's crooked or leaning, straighten it up. If it's rusting or dirty, shine it up. If it's old or dull, dress it up! Even painting it a shiny hunter green can be a big improvement over an old dirty box.

Remember, your mailbox may be the first thing house hunters see when they view your property—so make it something worth looking at!

▪ Bag the Boring Buzzer

Every house hunter spends a crucial moment standing at the front door of your home before it opens. What will your house hunters be looking at during that time? Will they be facing a cheap plastic doorbell or will they be looking at something attractive and unique that will be remembered?

If you've got one of those non-descript buzzers, it's usually pretty easy to take it apart and install something more decorative. There are so many different types of doorbells available these days. You can find them in gift shops, home supply stores, garden stores, local art fairs, museum shops and again, over the Internet. They come in ceramic, metal, glass, wrought iron and stone, in every color and theme to fit every style of home. Most of these can be installed within minutes using a little glue or a couple of screws.

If you've got a dramatic entrance to your home, a beautiful doorbell will make it look even better. But you do have to watch out though, because there are a lot of tacky doorbells out there. I've seen quite a few green frog doorbells that would actually cheapen the look of a home, unless of course, you lived next to a frog pond. So be careful to choose a bell that is tasteful instead of . . . um . . . tacky.

▪ Mind the Knob

If you've been living in your home for a number of years, your doorknob may have changed over time. It may not be the same shiny knob you remember when you first moved in. Over the years, through constant use, your knob may have accumulated a layer of gunk that you didn't see coming. Go outside and take a look.

I always advise people when they put their homes on the market to buy metal polish and give their doorknob a good cleaning. They are often surprised to see the rag they use turn black. They are even more surprised to see the difference it makes when it's clean.

If your doorknob is looking old, cheap, or beat-up, and no amount of polishing can make it look beautiful again, you might consider installing a new one. Of course, you will have to find a knob that fits the holes you already have in your door. But whether you polish it or replace it, having a shining doorknob is a great lead into your home.

▪ Get a Kick Out of Your Door

After years of using your front door, the bottom of it can get pretty dirty, scuffed, splintered, warped or even dented from people using their feet to kick or hold the door open as they enter and leave. Kids are famous for doing this, as are adults who use their feet to open the door when their hands are full of groceries.

However, you can make this liability into an asset by installing a shiny new metal kick plate across the bottom of your front door. Not only does it hide scuffs and dents, it makes your door look rich and more substantial. Even if your door is in good shape, adding a kick plate will make it look better.

You'll often see these plates on the doors of mansions, country clubs, and expensive doctor and lawyers' offices. Yet the price of a kick plate is surprisingly low. They are typically just a thin sheet of brass or steel that you can buy at a home improvement store or hardware store. But once installed, they make your entryway look richer.

Installing the kick plate is very easy too. All you need to do is attach the four little screws that come with it to your door. How easy is that?

▪ Match Your Door Mat

Here is another way to serve up some charm at the threshold of your home. Even if you have a condo in a high-rise building, you may be able to put out a doormat that adds a welcoming touch.

Now I hope you aren't visualizing one of those black rubber mats when I say this. There are many beautiful doormats available to suit any style home or environment. There are even metal mats with polished gold trim that look like works of art that you can step on. No matter what style your home is, there is a mat that will beautify your entrance. If you've got a double door entrance, there are four and five foot long mats to make a bigger statement.

If you've got a worn out welcome mat, this is a good time to say goodbye to it and welcome in a new one. Your mat is the first step a person makes to get into your home and the last step they take when leaving it. So there is no better place to put your best foot forward. By combining the effect of a nice mat, a polished door knob, a shiny kick plate and an attractive doorbell, you're definitely setting your house up to make a good first impression.

■ Put Out Some Pots

You can add instant color, style and life to your walkway or porch by putting out a variety of colorful pots filled with flowers or local plants. If you live in an area where deer, wild pigs, or other wildlife come around and eat your delicious foliage, ask the nursery staff to recommend plants that are wildlife resistant. If you live in an area of blistering summer heat, pick graceful local grasses that can withstand high temperatures and direct sun. If your house is on the market during winter, you might want to bring your plants in at night or on extremely cold days and put them back out only during showings.

If you live in a condo with an interior walkway, there's even a way to add potted plants to your indoor environment. If your building allows it, get a few nice looking pots and fill them with long, graceful dried reeds instead of flowers. This can make a beautiful frame around your door. (And, reeds look much classier than artificial flowers.)

If you're using live plants outdoors and don't want to stick your fingers in dirt, just pop the potted plant, container and all, into a decorative pot and you are done. However, you still have to water your plants so they don't die on you. Dead plants will only gain you red checkmarks.

■ Create a Viewing Perch

One of the great pastimes throughout the ages has been sitting outside the front of one's home, looking out at the world beyond. By setting out a small table and a couple of chairs, or even a colorful wooden bench, you can create a cozy vantage point for watching the world go by.

Imagine a little blue table and chairs in front of a white house, or a turquoise wooden bench with colorful pillows sitting on the porch of a yellow house. Now add a couple of ceramic pots spilling over with flowers and you've created the perfect porch scene. Not only is this set-up attractive, it addresses the natural human desire to be safely at home in one's own private world while comfortably spying on all the neighbors. This is one the main reasons porches were constructed in the first place. So if you're lucky enough to have a porch, use it to its fullest advantage.

■ Get The Grey Out

With a gallon or two of colored concrete stain and concrete varnish you can quickly turn dull grey patios, driveways and walkways into an attractive background that complements your entire home and makes it look more expensive.

Having done this to our own property, I can tell you the difference it makes. My husband and I transformed our grey patio floor into a beautiful outdoor room in about five hours, using just a couple of cans of concrete stain and varnish.

We were first considering tiling the patio, but when we discovered it would cost about $2,000 for just a small space, we opted for staining the concrete instead. For less than $100 we dramatically improved the look of our outdoor area, and the view from inside looked great as well.

Once I knew this trick, I started noticing others who had

done the same to their home exteriors. On neighborhood walks I would notice beautiful terra cotta colored porches, golden brown driveways and pretty brick red pathways. This little touch can bring a property's entire landscaping together, instead of looking like a home that sprung up out of a sea of grey cement.

You can hire someone to stain your concrete for you or you can do it yourself for much less. But, you'll need some knee-pads because this does take work. You'll also need to read the directions carefully to ensure you do it right!

▪ Attract Winged Things

A funny thing happens when you attract wildlife: you also attract people who are attracted by wildlife. House hunters are often charmed to see a property frequented by birds and butterflies. To get the butterflies to stick around your house, ask your local nursery experts which flowers are the most butterfly-friendly. Put a few pots of the stuff around your front entrance, or plant them along your walkway, then sit back and enjoy the visitors.

If you add a hummingbird feeder or two you can also enjoy a symphony of beating wings and high-pitched tweets. To attract a myriad of finches and songbirds that might be in your area, get a little bird feeder or simply put out a saucer of wild bird seed. It's amazing how quickly the word spreads around the animal kingdom that a new food source is available. (Just remember to tell the songbirds to keep it a secret from the pigeons.)

▪ Step Up in Style

Lead the way to your front door or through your yard using decorative stepping-stones. There are many varieties to choose from, including elegant pieces of slate or flagstone, brick, stamped concrete, or concrete embedded with stained glass in the shape of flowers, sunbursts, birds and butterflies. You can even find attractive recycled rubber stepping-stones featuring artistic designs.

It's also pretty easy to make your own concrete stones using a plastic mold and adding stained glass, marbles, or shells to fresh mixed concrete. If you would like to buy a stepping-stone making kit, take a look at sites such as http://www.milestonesproducts.com and http://www.yardlover.com, which feature many different types of stepping-stones.

■ Turn on the "Rock" Music

If you really want your home to be remembered and to give it a luxurious touch, get some outdoor speakers for your deck, patio or garden and turn on the music. If you've ever been to a high-end garden show, you'll see this done. As you walk through the picture-perfect display gardens you'll hear classical piano or soft jazz wafting through the flowers and trees. You'll think you've just stumbled into heaven.

You don't have to have a high-end garden however, to bring your music outdoors. There are plenty of inexpensive, easy-to-install outdoor speakers available, including speakers built right into the bottom of garden pots, wireless speakers, and speakers built into decorative artificial rocks. In fact, you can even pick the color and style of the rock you want!

These speakers cost around $50 to $200 or higher, depending upon the quality and sound range, and they are available through catalogs or online, at sites such as http://www.skymall.com, http://alloutdoorspeaker.com and http://www.stereostone.com.

Before a showing, just turn on some soft music and let your

house hunters enjoy. This is a great way to create a little outdoor paradise they won't easily forget. And, what's even better, you can take those speakers with you when you move on, unless they're included in the contract when you sell the house.

▪ Ring Your Chimes

Chimes are one of the fastest ways to create a sense of relaxation and peace in your outdoor environment. Hang them from trees, from your patio, or even from the overhang of a condo balcony. All it takes is a light breeze to create a sense of ease.

You do not have to stop at one set of chimes either. A combination of several tones generated from different sets of chimes in different locations can make a beautiful symphony. But you do have to be careful when choosing your chimes—some make a delightful tinkling sound, while others can be annoyingly noisy and clanky (leading to unhappy neighbors). So listen carefully to your chimes before buying them and make your decision based on the beauty of their tone.

▪ Add a Twinkle

Those little lights are not just for Christmas anymore! Strings of pinpoint lights look great throughout the year hanging on trees, decks, umbrellas, patios, gazebos and other outdoor structures. Somehow these little lights can't help but appeal to the little kid in all of us.

Your best bet is to stick with the little white bulbs, which add a festive touch without looking tacky, or as if you forgot to take down your Christmas lights. You can also purchase decorative strings of little lanterns, starbursts, dragonflies, boats, kites, chili peppers, or many other decorative lights to further add to the theme of your home or outdoor area. Turn these on for evening showings or on grey overcast days and you'll give your property an extra lift.

▪ Add a Tinkle

A small tinkling fountain next to your door or on your deck will bring a sense of tranquility to your property while adding visual appeal. If you don't have a power plug outside you can still do this. As long as there is sun, you can use a solar fountain and put it anywhere the sun shines.

Another option for incorporating calming water into your environment is to get a birdbath. Then you'll get the added benefit of birds and birdsong. Or, get a stone that has been carved out to create a bowl that holds water. You can often find these at nurseries and statuary stores, and they look fantastic holding a single flower floating on water.

▪ Create an Instant Outdoor Room

Here's an easy way to add an outdoor dining room or shaded lounging spot to your house for around $100: set up a portable tented gazebo. You can often find these gazebos-in-a-box at stores such as Target and Costco, and you can put them up in very little time.

Assemble your gazebo anywhere you have about ten square feet of space available, wrap a string of lights around it, and you've got a surprisingly attractive centerpiece for your yard! A gazebo also helps house hunters better envision the amount of space and uses there are for your outdoor area. As long as your gazebo isn't permanently installed on your property and it isn't part of your home sale contract, you can also fold it up and take it with you when you move.

■ Open Up a Bright Umbrella

If you don't have a patio or gazebo, another way to add shade and color to your yard is to put up a big umbrella. Then add a table, a couple of chairs and a few pots of flowers and you've made it easy for house hunters to see themselves enjoying your outdoor space.

■ Plant Something Unexpected

Give your garden a whimsical, creative touch by planting a couple of unexpected objects among your flowers, trees and bushes. Sculptures, colorfully painted watering cans, wrought iron benches, even an antique brightly painted bicycle can give your garden a curious appeal when planted in the midst of your daisies or rose bushes.

You'll find a wealth of interesting odds and ends at flea markets, thrift stores and garage sales that will cost you very little, but can add a jolt of unexpected charm. All you need is one colorful object, such as an old iron chair, spray painted bright red with a bright yellow pot of flowers on it, to make your garden more interesting and memorable.

■ Create Multiple Sitting Zones

My retired friend Harry is the master of creating distinct sitting zones all around the outside of his home to catch the different hours of sunlight and shade. Even the pathways on the sides of his home have been lined with beautiful stepping-stones, pots of flowers, and places to lounge.

By creating these little zones, Harry says he never gets bored of just hanging out in his own backyard. He takes his morning coffee in one zone, naps in his hammock in another, eats lunch in a third, and enjoys cocktails in the evening while watching the sunset from another spot.

What's amazing is that Harry's property isn't very large—it's just that he's designed his outdoor space in such a way that it feels as if you've got numerous places to go. What's even more amazing is that Harry created all of this using just a few materials such as stones and pebbles of various sizes, shrubs, potted plants, and some strategically placed furniture and trellises. The biggest component, Harry said, was adding creativity.

Rather than seeing your property as only a front yard and a back yard, consider how you can creatively divide your space into multiple outdoor "rooms." By doing this, you can create impressive, usable spaces that house hunters will love.

How to Eliminate Red Checkmarks Outside Your Home

As a seller you need to constantly be on the lookout for all the little things that can go wrong outside your door. The best way to find these things is to walk around your property frequently with the eyes of a first-time visitor.

Here are some tips for eliminating potential red checkmarks:

▪ Don't Display Garbage Cans

Garbage cans, no matter how clean and functional they may be, are just not alluring home features. Keep them away from the front or sides of your house and store them in your garage or a tool shed if possible. If it's garbage day and you must have them out, get them off the street and back in their hiding places as soon as you can.

▪ Remove Dying Plants

Plants in poor health automatically distract from an attractive entryway, making it look a little sad. If you want to nurse a sick plant back to life, try to do it somewhere far away from your front door. You may be able to transplant it to another location where it has a better chance of getting the sun, shade or soil type it needs.

The gardener for our old house in Arizona taught us this. We had a series of tall attractive green shrubs right outside the front door that were turning into crispy brown sticks because of the relentless desert sun. We thought they were goners, but the gardener dug them up and replanted them in a shady spot behind the house where they flourished and made the backyard look great.

▪ Make Your Lawn a Green Carpet

If a lawn is overgrown, patchy or dying, it immediately sends the signal that your house is unloved. House hunters will think to themselves, "If the house looks like this on the outside, it's probably not much better on the inside." From that moment on, they'll be on the lookout for other negative aspects of your house to confirm this opinion. That's why first impressions are critical. A beautiful front lawn sends the signal that your entire home is well cared for.

▪ Get Rid of Weeds and Dead Leaves

Sometimes all it takes is a few big thorny weeds that pop up overnight to give potential buyers the idea that they should knock $5,000 off their offer price. Any sign that your home is uncared for can make potential buyers think you're in a desperate situation and willing to sell for less. That's why it's important to constantly remove weeds and dead leaves so you don't accidentally signal "desperation."

▪ Don't Show Off Ugly Cars

Let's face it, having a shiny new Mercedes in front of your house gives a better first impression than an old clunker. If you have an old car, or even a dirty car, it's best not to park it in your driveway. It's another signal to potential homebuyers that you might not be taking good care of your possessions, including your home. It also sends the signal that you might be willing to accept less for your house because you might be financially struggling.

So if your car is dirty or not in the best shape, park it down the street if you can. (It's better to keep it out of your garage too.) However, if you have a shiny old classic Corvette, that's another story. Feel free to park that car right in front of your house. Assumptions can work to your advantage as well.

▪ Fix Cracks and Peeling Paint

While you're walking around your house looking for weeds and dead leaves, keep your eyes out for cracks, peeling paint, dirt, dust and cobwebs on your walls, overhangs and windows. The more maintained your home looks, the more it will appear easy for a new owner to keep it that way, further improving your chance of an offer.

▪ Straighten Anything Crooked

Think of all the scary movies you've ever seen. A tell-tale sign of a decrepit house is a crooked fence, lamppost, gate or mailbox. These things give people the creeps, even though you might not have noticed them because they've grown crooked over time. But house hunters will take note and can get scared away. That's why it's important to make sure anything that leans is standing up straight and ready to welcome a new buyer.

▪ Pitch the Procrastination Collections

Most everyone has them—things that accumulate around the sides or back of your property that you don't know what to do with . . . broken tiles that you don't want to throw out, (because you might make a mosaic out of them someday) a tool that needs fixing, plastic gardening pots that you might reuse, or a half bag of soil that you're going to bring over to your neighbors (when you're both home at the same time).

The trouble with these things is that they look messy and often become a gathering place for weeds, dead leaves, spiders and even snakes. If you want to give your home's perimeter a quick lift, find a new home for these miscellaneous items today!

▪ Sweep Your Surfaces

Keep your pathways, porch, patio, and any other horizontal surfaces around your property free of floating debris. It collects quickly, but engaging in frequent sweeping motions will not only eliminate red checkmarks, it burns calories too.

CHAPTER SEVEN

How To Get Your Home Ready to Show in 10 Minutes or Less

The phone rings. Someone wants to see your house. You look around and see messes everywhere, like little brush fires across a vast landscape. The newspaper is spread out on the kitchen table, a half a loaf of French bread is sitting on the countertop surrounded by a sea of crumbs, your laundry is sprawled across the floor, and your credit card bill and jewelry are on top of your dusty dresser.

You ask if the house hunters can come in a couple of hours, but you find out they're only going to be in your area for a short time. So you stop everything and embark on a massive cleanup operation while the clock ticks away. You hide all your sensitive documents, expensive possessions, and tuck the French bread in your bottom drawer. You'll look for it later and hope you remember where you put it all.

When you finish cleaning and stashing, you're exhausted, stressed out, and a little frustrated because you know there is a good chance you'll never hear back from these house hunters again.

After the showing you forget about the bread for a week and eventually find it rock-hard in the bottom drawer. But you still can't remember where you hid your credit card bill. (Where did you put that again?)

That's how it used to be when I got a call for a showing. After too many experiences like this, I decided to create a system that would help me clean and organize my house quickly. So I created a written checklist of tasks to do before every showing. I also established some simple steps to keep my house looking better on a daily basis. It worked. I was able to cut my cleaning time down to about 10 minutes and I never lost a thing again.

Here's how I did it:

There really is no way around it. If you want to clean up your house lightning-fast, you've got to keep it somewhat clean on a daily basis. But this doesn't have to be difficult.

House cleaning follows the laws of physics, specifically the laws of momentum and inertia. If a place is messy, it's easier to make it messier. For example, take your kitchen countertop—if it's sparkling clean with nothing on it, you'll probably put your latest dirty dish in the dishwasher instead of leaving it on your clean countertop. However, if you've already got dirty dishes accumulating there, it's much easier to add another—what's one more? So the law of physics states that dirty dishes attract more dirty dishes. And so it goes throughout your house.

The best way to keep things clean is to make a game out of it. Whenever you enter a room, look for *one* thing you can clean quickly or put away in a minute or so. If you walk in the bathroom, give the mirror a quick swipe. Before leaving the kitchen, clean the crumbs around the toaster. When you step out on the front porch, pick up a few leaves. By doing this, your house is constantly being micro-cleaned.

Then once a week do an overall cleaning inside and out. Vacuum the rugs and dust off the windows, mirrors and ledges. Beat back any piles of papers that are accumulating. Check to make sure your garage has not become a hazardous waste dump. Mow the lawn so that your grass remains shorter than your roofline and sweep your patio and walkways.

Check for anything that might have died on your property, whether it's a plant or a bug, and make sure that everything around your house is standing up straight, including your "For Sale" sign. If you've got a flyer box outside advertising your home, keep it well stocked with fresh clean flyers.

By doing these tasks often, you never end up needing to do a heart-attack inducing top-to-bottom cleaning right before a showing. However, because you do live in your house and might not want to store everything the minute after you use it, you need a system to quickly hide the things that accumulate on your exposed surfaces. The following hide-away system will help you do that.

Create a Hide-Away System

In order to have a place to quickly stash your things, you first need to create dedicated hiding spots all over your house. Depending upon the room, your official hiding spot can be a drawer, a stack of attractive hatboxes, or an antique trunk.

Once you've created your hiding spots, make a list of what you want to hide and where you're going to put it, so you don't have to hunt for your things later. In case you're hiding expensive items, you might want to put them in a locked home safe, or at least cover them up with other things inside your drawers. In the kitchen, you can dedicate an empty cupboard shelf for stashing the things that normally sit on top of your kitchen counter, such as spotted bananas and vitamin bottles.

In your bathroom, clear out a drawer or use a box under the sink to stick items such as toothbrushes, toothpaste, and anything else that looks messy but usually sits on your countertop. In your office, designate a drawer for stashing your bills, paperwork and unopened mail.

Before a showing, simply put away everything on your checklist in their predetermined places.

Checklist of To-Do's Before Every Showing

If you keep your house fairly clean on a daily basis you can reduce your tasks down to a short, organized list. Here are the tasks I recommend doing before showings, and I've left spaces at the end of each section for you to write down any additional tasks you might want to do.

General Tasks

❑ Empty trashcans and put recycling material in garage (hide trashcans if possible)

❑ Sweep or wipe down any dirty surfaces

❑ Check for odors anywhere in the house

❑ Open windows and curtains if appropriate (or close windows and curtains if necessary)

❑ Turn on lights to highlight areas and illuminate gloomy spots

❑ Turn on air conditioning or heating as necessary

❑ Turn on decorative water fountains, add water if necessary

❑ Stash paperwork, bills and piles of papers in their hiding spots

❑ Stash valuable items such as jewelry, electronic devices, and small expensive possessions in their hiding spots

❑ Hide kids' toys

❑ Stash medicine and vitamin bottles
❑ Tuck in chairs, straighten furniture and pillows
❑ Hang a sign, if appropriate, to remind real estate agents and visitors to lock your back and side doors after the showing
❑ Additional tasks:

Kitchen

❑ Stash items on countertop in hiding places
❑ Empty trash and hide the can if possible
❑ Change your kitchen towel(s) if necessary
❑ Check countertops, sink, appliances and floor for cleanliness
❑ Additional tasks:

Living Room/Dining Room/Family Room

❑ Put away newspapers and items that have accumulated on your furniture or other surfaces
❑ Dust any surfaces that need it
❑ Additional tasks:

Bathrooms

- ❏ Clean and dry mirrors, sinks, tub and/or shower
- ❏ Put toilet lids down
- ❏ Put away items around the sink area, such as toothpaste, toothbrushes, dental floss, shaving supplies, cosmetics, and pill bottles in pre-determined hiding places
- ❏ Check towels for cleanliness or put out "show" towels
- ❏ Empty garbage from cans
- ❏ Additional tasks:

Bedrooms

- ❏ Put away your valuables
- ❏ Put away stray clothes or belongings
- ❏ Make all the beds and organize pillows
- ❏ Additional tasks:

Office/Study

- ❏ Put away valuables and paperwork
- ❏ Lock file cabinets if necessary
- ❏ Turn off computer if confidential information can be easily viewed
- ❏ Additional tasks:

Pets

- ❏ Clean or hide cat box and cat litter supplies
- ❏ Clean area around pet food bowl
- ❏ Stash pet toys
- ❏ Get pets ready to go if you plan to take them with you during a showing, or secure them in a safe place during the showing
- ❏ Additional tasks:

Outside Areas

- ❏ Check porch, entryway, walkways and doormat for cleanliness. Scan for any dead leaves, bugs or trash that may have blown onto your property
- ❏ Put away garbage cans
- ❏ Clean areas frequented by dogs
- ❏ Pull out any big ugly weeds that may have popped up along the sides of your home
- ❏ Additional tasks:

During The Showing

This is the time to reward yourself for your cleaning and upkeep. If you do not have to be present at your home showing, go out somewhere and relax. Get a cup of coffee, visit friends, or take a leisurely hike, knowing you deserve the break.

After The Showing

**After the showing there is
another checklist of things to do:**

- ❑ Turn off lights, air conditioning or heating that you turned on for the showing
- ❑ Check back doors, sliding glass doors and windows to see if they are locked
- ❑ Pull out important paperwork, bills or expensive items from their hiding places if you need them
- ❑ Bring out the cat box from hiding (if you have a cat). Bring in pets that may have been put away during the showing
- ❑ Bring out hidden food items from their hiding places
- ❑ Bring out DVDs and books that need to be returned to a rental store or library
- ❑ Check for signs that show someone was seated on your couch or chairs. This might be a sign that they were interested enough in your house to sit down and think about it!
- ❑ If you have a real estate agent, ask for feedback on the home showing. What did the visitors like? What did they have concerns over? Note negative comments such as "the price is too high" or any other feedback that you may want to address.
- ❑ Based upon feedback, make changes as necessary
- ❑ Additional tasks:

By establishing good cleaning and organization habits, you can eliminate a great deal of the stress involved in having your home on the market. At least you'll never have to worry about cleaning frantically before a surprise showing. And, you can leave your house anytime you want without worrying that someone might come by and find it dirty. In addition, you'll probably find that a clean, organized home is a more relaxing, pleasurable environment to live in.

What To Do About Pets

When we first put our house on the market this was a real bugaboo, as it is for many people with beloved canines, felines, bovines and porcupines. If you leave your pet in the house they may run out when the door opens, no matter how hard a real estate agent or buyer tries to keep them inside. You may also not want to leave them in your home or yard for a variety of reasons. (Especially the bovines and porcupines.) So what can you do?

Here are several ideas: if you have a neighbor or friend in the area, ask if they would hold on to your pet during the house tour in exchange for babysitting their pets at another time. There are also doggie daycare sites popping up in many cities where you can leave your pooch for just a few hours. (Just check on their requirements before you drop them off for the first time. Many of them require proof of pet vaccinations.)

Another option, which allows you to keep your pet at home, is to put them along with their food, water and necessities in a room in your house that is the least important (such as a bonus or storage room). Just install a lock that lets you lock the door with a key from the outside, and then place a few attractive photos of the room on the door along with its dimensions so visitors can see exactly what the interior looks like. Also explain that your pet is inside for safekeeping and that visitors are invited to come back again if they would like to see this room. If a house hunter is interested, this provides them with another reason to come back a second time, which is always a good sign for a home seller.

We did this in our house because we didn't want to take the chance of our cat escaping in an area known for coyotes. So we hired a locksmith to install a locking door in an unfinished room in our basement, and then we made it into a cozy cat haven. This way we knew our pet was safe—and we did have several interested visitors who came back a second time to see the "mystery" room.

CHAPTER EIGHT

The Good News About Not Selling Your House Quickly

When we had our house on the market for months and months, I began looking for the silver lining to keep from going crazy. When I looked closer, I found a dozen positive things about being stuck with our house. It's important to keep these things in mind and take full advantage of them, because they will make the waiting period *so* much better.

■ You Get to Live in Your House at its Best

Many times I've heard people who sold their house say, "I've finally made my house look the way I've always wanted and now I have to leave it all behind." Think about all the hard work, cleaning and beautiful touches you've added. You've made the yard look great, the rooms feel comfortable and organized, and the master bathroom looks as if it belongs in a spa. So now is the time, while you're waiting to sell, to really "live" in your house.

Enjoy the clean, spacious rooms, sip tea in your garden, and kick back and read a book in a house that looks like a showplace. If it takes a while for your house to sell, it means you've got a little more precious time to enjoy it. Because once it's gone, it's gone for good.

■ You've Got a Good Excuse for Getting a Few Frills

Normally you might feel a bit guilty purchasing fancy towels and shower curtains, decorative pillows and outdoor stereo speakers. But now that you're trying to sell your house you have a good excuse for purchasing some of these niceties. These little luxuries might end up selling your house for you.

Part of the enjoyment is the shopping experience itself. You get to go out looking for beautiful things that will bring your house alive, and once it sells, a lot of it gets to come with you!

■ You've Got Time (and Motivation) to Take Classes

If you've ever wanted to take a class in photography, interior design, outdoor sculpture making, faux wall painting or gardening . . . the time is now. Not only will you be learning a new enjoyable skill that will get you out of the house, you can use your skills to enhance your surroundings.

When my friend Joanne had her house on the market, she took a mosaic class and learned to make her own concrete stepping-stones embedded with stained glass. Not only did the class distract her from her worries, she created a gorgeous pathway that meandered through her garden. (She also got to take the stepping-stones with her when she moved.)

There also seems to be some sort of mystical power in *not* staying home and waiting endlessly for your circumstances to change. It's like the old saying, "a watched pot never boils."

Just the act of getting out of your house and keeping busy might help bring a buyer to your door!

■ It's Easier to Invite Visitors Over

When the house is a mess it's less likely you'll invite visitors over. And if it's a real mess, you probably don't want to put in all the effort to clean it anyway, so dinner guests will be few and far between. But if your house is always on the verge of being spotless, inviting people over for impromptu gatherings is easy and fun.

You just need to take the newspaper off the table, set out the cheese and crackers and let the good times roll. And, if you want to cook something up, you'll have a lot more energy because you don't have to clean up the whole house first. It's enough to make you consider keeping your house clean for good.

■ You Get Extra Time to Organize and Pack

One of the big stresses of moving is having to organize all of your family's possessions under time pressure before the sale closes. This is especially true when your house sells quickly and you've got to get out fast. You might have only 30 or 40 days to pack up everything you've accumulated over the last 10 or 20 years.

As a result, a lot of unnecessary items come with you to your new home because you didn't have time to throw them out. Instead, you end up dumping the contents of your drawers straight into a box—or maybe you just bring your drawers filled with old things directly to your new location.

But if you have months and months of waiting time, you

can eliminate the last-minute packing pressure. Every week you can devote a little time to culling through your garage, closets and drawers, figuring out what to throw out, give away or take with you. So when your house does sell, all you have to do is pack up the things you want and start fresh.

■ You Learn You Don't Really Need That Much

Once you clear your kitchen, bathroom, closets and garage of miscellaneous doo-dads, you realize you never really needed all that stuff in the first place. Maybe in the beginning, as you pack it away, you'll get a momentary pang of sadness, but soon you won't even miss the stuff.

For most of us, our belongings follow the "80/20" rule: 20% of our belongings get 80% of the usage, while 80% are used only 20% of the time, and often much less. In fact, we use a lot of our things 0% of the time.

Once all of this extra fluff is gone, you'll find the things that you really want to keep seem much more precious to you. For one thing, you'll know where it all is. I can't tell you how many nice shirts I've found in my closet once I isolated them from all the unwanted clothes that hid them from view.

But it's not just your possessions that will seem more precious: your entire house will feel lighter—and so will your spirits. There is something very important to be said about losing hundreds, or maybe even thousands of pounds of dead weight!

■ You Grow Accustomed to New Organizational Habits

Once you see how good it feels to have a sparkling kitchen, uncluttered surfaces and organized closets, it's easy to grow fond of this lifestyle. Also, maintaining it this way is much easier when all you have to do is swipe a rag across a countertop, instead of having to figure out where to put a foot-tall stack of papers.

By keeping your house clean for possible showings, you train yourself to be a neater, more organized person. You begin to do amazing things like opening your bank statements immediately upon receiving them and then putting them in a pre-determined location. Not only does this keep your home tidy, it eliminates the chronic anxiety that comes from living in a state of chaos and disorganization.

Behaviorists say that it typically takes around 21 consistent days to form a habit. When your house is on the market for months and months, you have plenty of time to create new organizational habits that you get to take with you when you move. And what's even better, you don't even have to set a New Year's resolution to do this. All you have to do is put your house on the market and have it not sell for a while. (How's that for looking for the silver lining?)

▪ You Get Continuous Exercise

When you are constantly in motion cleaning, sweeping, scrubbing and weeding, you accidentally burn a lot of calories. Add to this, a lot of lifting, stooping, squatting and reaching, and you can start losing pounds without forgoing cookies.

As you are performing these constant little moves, remember you're getting free exercise without having to go to a gym or do 50 boring sit-ups each morning. I once read about a scientific study conducted using hotel maids. The study said that maids who were aware of the fact that they were getting exercise while performing their daily duties were much happier, and actually lost more weight than the maids who didn't think about the calories they were burning.

The moral of this story is to notice all the little cleaning acts you do and realize that they not only keep your house clean—they keep you lean!

■ You Get Time to Adjust to the Fact That You Really Are Moving

One of the difficulties of getting an offer on your house immediately after putting it on the market is that you don't have time to mentally adjust to the truth that you really are going to move. You might not be psychologically ready for such a massive change.

I've had this happen, and it felt very unsettling. We put the house on the market on Friday afternoon and before the weekend was over, another family was trying to figure out how to move their king size bed up our staircase.

It felt as if the house was being pulled right out from underneath me. And it made me wonder if I was crazy for wanting to leave it. After all, if someone else wanted my house that badly, maybe I was missing something. Maybe I was crazy for wanting to give up my lifestyle.

All of these things were circulating through my head as I began packing up my possessions under tremendous time pressure. Looking at the excitement on the new buyers' faces when they came by to covet *their* new home just made me feel all the worse.

None of this happens, however, if you've been waiting to sell your house for months or years. Instead you feel the opposite: finally, someone is taking your poor, rejected house off your hands! Finally you can move on with your life. Finally, you get to CELEBRATE!

■ You Are Forced Into Living in the Moment

When you can't make things happen exactly *when* and *how* you want them to, your personality subtly begins to change. You grow to accept the fact that you can't always be in full control. You simultaneously begin to realize the world is filled with options and alternatives, and that you can make your life flow like a river around obstacles, instead of trying to blast your way right through them.

Maybe instead of selling your home, you rent it out. Or, you decide to stay and find ways to make it work for you. Or, you lower your price beyond what you previously thought you would and you make peace with that decision.

Although this may feel as if you're in a compromising position, it actually shows you how free you are to bend and change, and that there is always another way. Instead of feeling out of control, you realize that ultimately you're in control of how you think and adjust to any situation you're faced with. This is a true gift, wrapped in what at first glance appears to be an extremely difficult situation.

■ You've Got Extra Time To Explore Your Area

You've probably said this to yourself: "One day I want to go to that place." You might be talking about a local restaurant, a park, a store, a hiking area, or a museum. You keep driving by it or reading about it, but for some reason you just haven't gotten around to going there yet.

If you sell your house quickly, you probably will never get

around to going there. You'll be too busy packing up to even think about it. And if you move out of the area, the chance of visiting those places drops to almost zero.

But if your house is on the market for an extended period of time, this is an opportunity to go out exploring! Make a list of all those places you've wanted to see and start crossing them off one by one. You've got the luxury of time right now while your house is sitting on the market, so the more extra days you have, the more things you can try out.

■ You've Got a Good Excuse to Eat Out

You've just cleaned every inch of your countertops, swept up the crumbs, wiped up the sink, cleaned the stovetop, removed all the refrigerator fingerprints, and polished the microwave. And now you're hungry. This is a good time to have lunch at that Chinese buffet you've been meaning to try or grab some sandwiches at the market and go for a picnic. This is especially true if you're getting ready for a showing. Who wants to mess up a perfectly clean kitchen? You really do have a great excuse for enjoying a relaxing meal somewhere else.

CHAPTER NINE

Beating the Home Seller's Blues

Of all the proverbs I've ever heard, the most profound is this:

"Pain is inevitable in life, but suffering is optional."

How true this is. We don't have control over the inevitability of experiencing painful events, but we do have control over how we choose to handle them. We can moan and groan and feel like helpless victims, or we can figure out how to redirect, reinterpret and transform painful experiences into something more positive.

As a home seller it's important to have an arsenal of tools to help you transform your anxiety, frustration and doubt into actions that will not only eliminate suffering, but make this period in your life a lot more fun and fruitful.

Here is a list of ways to beat the Home Seller's Blues:

■ Ask Yourself: What's the Worst That Can Happen?

Let's get the hardest one over with first: with anything difficult that you have to go through, it's wise to face it head-on and ask yourself, "What's the worst that can happen?" Even though this question seems scary, it's even scarier to live in the unknown, trying not to think about some formless, nameless, horrible threat that is out there waiting for you.

It's like feeling something is lurking outside your window at night, but being too afraid to look out and see what it is. But once you know, you can take action and do something about it. Most of the time, you'll find out that it's not as bad as you thought. What you imagined was a vampire with long fingernails scraping against your windowpane is actually just a skinny tree branch that you can easily trim in the morning.

When it comes to home selling, the obvious worst thing that can happen is not being able to pay your bills and losing your house. As tragic as this is, people still survive and get on with the next chapter in their lives. However, there is also a good chance that you won't get to this point. It's a lot like falling down a hill. You don't necessarily fall all the way to the bottom. There are usually stopping places along the way where you can catch yourself. When it comes to selling your home, it's the same. There are a lot of resources and options out there that can help keep the worst from happening.

The important thing to realize is that even if the worst happens, you'll figure out how to handle it and live through it. Think about your life up until now—haven't you always figured out ways to get by? If you've done it up until now, who says you won't be able to handle this one too?

Even though the worst may never happen, it's still a good idea to examine your fears instead of being afraid to even consider them. By doing this, you will connect with your inner strength, as well as possible solutions.

▪ Ask Yourself: What's the Best That Can Happen?

Okay, you've asked yourself about the worst, now look at it from the other side and ask, "What's the *best* that can happen?" A lot of us aren't in the habit of doing this. Our minds tend to dwell on potential negative outcomes, rather than focusing on possible good ones. This is truly unfortunate because if you think about it, good things are constantly happening to us just as much or more than the bad things.

Even events we consider negative often have positive benefits. For example, you don't get the job, date or house you want, but instead you end up finding a better, more suitable job, date or house.

As I write this, I think about my friend Angela, a massage therapist who lost her lease on a home that doubled as her workspace and living area. At first she was distraught. She loved her place, even though her clients had to walk through the house to get to her massage room. She figured she would never find such a nice, well-located rental for such a great price again. But when she went looking, she actually found something better: a home close to all of her clients with its own separate studio and beautiful courtyard to use as a waiting area. The house also had a sauna and a hot tub, plus it was almost the same price as her first place! So, even though Angela lost her lease and had to move out, things turned out much better than she ever expected.

Now ask yourself, what positive outcomes can accidentally come out of not being able to sell your home? Is it possible that an opportunity can come your way because you are "stuck" where you are? Could you accidentally find a new career, job, best friend or a new mate because of your current situation? It might even be possible that this positive outcome shifts your circumstances so that you don't want to, or have to sell your house.

■ Realize the Outcome Will Probably Be Somewhere in the Middle

Now that you've considered the worst thing that can happen and the best, chances are that your outcome will be somewhere in the middle (which isn't so bad, really). Most likely you won't be cast out on the street, but you won't have sold your house overnight for the highest possible price either. Chances are you'll probably find a creative outcome somewhere in the middle that you can live with. This should make it at least a little easier to sleep at night.

■ Write Down Your Feelings

I know some of you might be saying, "I'm not the expressive type, or I'm not the writing type, or I'm not the typing type." But the fact is, there have been plenty of scientific experiments involving human beings (and not just lab mice) who have been instructed to keep a personal journal of their thoughts and worries, and found the practice tremendously comforting.

Studies have shown that people who keep a daily journal often feel better both mentally and physically than those who hold it all in. By writing, you give yourself time and space to think through your feelings. It also makes it easier to think through the possible decisions you can make.

In addition, many people believe that writing is the best

way to get to the truth of how they *really* feel, because it's much harder to lie to yourself on paper. Any untruth you try to tell yourself sticks out like a sore thumb when you write it down. As a result, all this truth-telling can lead to insights and actions that you might not have otherwise considered.

So do yourself a big favor. Get out a pen and paper and write down what you're going through. Write down your fears, worries and your symptoms of Home Seller's Blues. Take a deep breath and let it all out. Then write down the hopes and dreams you have for a brighter future. Do this regularly and you'll see the change it will make in you. You'll agree with 9 out of 10 lab mice and humans—writing makes you feel much better.

■ Make A Clear, Calm, Decision (For Now)

It's not unusual to go back and forth between possible decisions that you could make. Should you reduce your property price for a quicker sale? Should you take your home off the market? Should you run off to Mexico and open a juice bar or give up everything and join a nunnery or a circus? Living in indecision can make you crazy.

To give yourself peace of mind, there are really only three main choices to choose from, and you already know what they are: you can lower the price of your property and do everything you can to make your home sell. You can offer your home at the price you want and be prepared to wait it out. Or, you can take your home off the market and find a way to pay your bills. Of these three, which feels best to you?

Make a choice and make peace with it. You don't have to live with this decision for the rest of your life, but at least stick to it for several months to give yourself a break from non-stop doubt and indecision. You can always reevaluate your situation and change your course when you've gathered new information.

The beauty of making a single, clear, calm decision is that it helps you focus and illuminate one particular path. This is much better than trying to keep all options open and never being able to move forward in any one direction.

▪ Give Yourself 20 Minutes of Dedicated Worrying

Rather than let worries continuously nip at your heels all day long, make it a habit to worry for 20 focused minutes per day at a convenient, specified time. Take this time to completely concentrate and luxuriate in all the things that concern you. (You might even want to write down a laundry list of your worries.)

Because we don't usually do this, our worries seem all-encompassing and insurmountable. But when we corral them together and stare them down as a group, they feel much more organized. You may find that you don't have quite as many worries as you thought. For example, you may think you have over 100, but when you sit down and list them all, you find you only have 78!

Writing down all of your concerns is similar to writing out a grocery list to go shopping after work. If you don't keep a list, you end up silently reminding yourself about what you need all day long. ("Don't forget the broccoli!") But, if you write it down, you can forget about it and concentrate on other things. The same goes with worries. If you write them down and know that you're going to deal with them later, you won't have to keep reminding yourself every hour!

Are you worried that this idea won't work? Just add it to your worry list and give it a try anyway. It might just make you feel better.

▪ Take a Complete Day Off From Worry

If the 20 minutes a day worry plan doesn't work for you (and even if it does), you might want to take an occasional break from fretting altogether. As stimulating and dynamic as worrying might be, it gets old when you do it too much.

If you can, get out of town into new surroundings, away from where your worry is centralized. If you live in a city, go out into nature. If you live around nature, visit a bustling nearby city where you can get absorbed in new surroundings. But whatever you do, try to get out of the house for the day.

Start off your worry-free day by imagining you are exhaling all your concerns into a big red balloon. Watch it get bigger and bigger. Now tie a knot and give it a tap, sending it skyward. Say goodbye to your worries and watch them rise further and further away, until the balloon disappears completely. Don't worry though. It isn't gone for good. It will come back down at the end of the day.

Now that you've sent your balloon packing, it's time to have a great day doing something completely different. If at any time you discover yourself worrying, give the balloon another tap and send it soaring again. If your day out includes other family members, make it a game to *not* talk about your problems during the entire time. If someone brings up a worry, he or she has to buy the other one lunch. (And no one can even bring up the thought of house selling.)

The goal is to get completely absorbed in the present moment. If you're out having coffee, be fully present with the coffee. If you're walking through a museum, be fully present with the art. If you meet new people, don't tell them about your home selling problems. Instead absorb yourself in their lives, or even find out what their challenges might be. You might enjoy your worry-free day so much that you'll decide to make it a weekly or monthly habit.

■ Don't Take House Rejection Personally!

After a showing it's understandable that you'll be itching for feedback. However, any response other than an outright offer can be misinterpreted as an insult. It's easy to think that people don't like your house, or they don't like your décor, or maybe they don't like the vibes of your house—all of which you can start taking a little personally. These feelings can compound as the months go by, especially if you discover that other houses in your area are selling, but not yours.

If you find yourself taking rejection personally, you need to remember that this isn't about *you*. House hunting is a lot like looking for the right pair of shoes. You might find a pair that looks great, and even comes in your favorite color and style, but if they don't fit, you aren't going to buy them.

The same goes for picking a house. If it doesn't fit what a buyer needs, he or she isn't going to choose it, no matter how great it looks. It has nothing to do with you or your vibes or your décor. Remember, you chose your house once, so chances are someone else will feel the same way you did when you bought it. To that person, your place will be the perfect fit.

■ Change Your Viewpoint About Living with Uncertainty

Uncertainty has got a bad rap. We usually think of it as uncomfortable and anxiety provoking. But there is another way to interpret uncertainty, and that is to view it as living in a state of surprise and wonderment.

After all, why do people like wrapped gifts? It's because we like the anticipation and the element of surprise. It makes us feel alive! Why don't we want to know how a movie ends before we see it? Again, we like the element of surprise. It's a lot more fun *not* to know what's going to happen next.

But when our homes are on the market and we don't know what's going to happen next? We don't like that too much. We need to remind ourselves that during this time, we are actually living a life of adventure and mystery, rather than anxiety-provoking misery. After all, we never know when the house is going to sell, for how much, and when exactly our lives are going to change. We have no idea when a long-awaited buyer is going to show up at the front door and make us an offer. And we never know until the very second it happens.

I remember the moment before the phone call announcing that my husband and I had received a good offer on the house that we had been trying to sell for a year: I was eating cereal and researching weekend activities in the newspaper. And then suddenly, BAM, everything changed. From that moment on our lives went hurtling off in a new direction. It was a giant gift-wrapped surprise.

And that's how it happens for all of us. So you might as well figure out how to enjoy living in a state of wonderment and anticipation instead of slogging along in glum uncertainty.

▪ Reclarify Your Worth

Is one of your concerns about not selling your house the fear that you won't be able to pay your bills? If so, you're in good company. But could it be that you're underestimating your worth? Could it be that you are selling yourself short and that you have talents that you aren't recognizing?

This might be something very important for you to look at, especially if the main reason you're selling your property is because of money issues. If so, this may be a great time to seriously look at some of the other things you can be doing to bring in extra income.

Could you be good at clothing alterations, photography, website writing, video production, tutoring, catering, fixing computer systems or selling used tripods on eBay? There are literally thousands of things you can do to supplement your income. You might be on the doorstep of discovering a new career that you'll love, and there is no better time to begin than when you are backed into a corner.

I read that Galileo came up with some of his most important inventions because he needed more money. Someone in his family got sick, so he'd invent something to help pay the bills. Throughout history, whenever mankind has been backed into a corner—that's when personal achievement happens. That's how almost every happy movie ends: The hero faces insurmountable odds and then pulls off something wonderful.

Nowadays, it's even easier to get started in many businesses because we can often do it while sitting in a chair in our underwear in front of a computer. So if there aren't many jobs in your area, you may still be able to derive your income over the Internet. In fact, many businesses require a national or international audience base to get enough interested customers to achieve success, which you can now reach no matter where you live.

Or, you might find that the thing you like to do can be done in your own backyard, or maybe your neighbors'. For example, one businesswoman in my area is growing 10' by

10' organic gardens in her neighbors' yards. Her business is exploding and it's the thing she loves to do the very most in the world!

So do *not* underestimate your value. This might be the perfect time to undergo your own personal renaissance.

▪ Keep Yourself Engaged

When your house is on the market, and especially if you're planning to move out of the area, it's easy to start disengaging from your current life. You might not want to get involved in community groups and events, or make new friends, or start projects that will last several months. Why put energy into something that you'll have to abandon once your house sells?

Shutting down on activities is the recipe for depression. It puts you in a situation where you aren't really living your current life, but aren't living your future life either. You can find yourself living in this state of limbo for months—feeling bored, isolated, and increasingly negative. On top of all of that, it gives you more time to fully develop the Home Seller's Blues.

Don't let this happen! Until your house is packed up and ready to load on a truck, do not unplug your life. Keep yourself locally engaged. Go to places you haven't been, join new groups, sign up for classes, make new friends, and seek out interesting opportunities.

Act as if you are planning to stay for a long while. This way, even if you don't sell your house for years, you're still living a happy life. You might even come across a brilliant opportunity that makes you want to stay right where you are now.

▪ Play With Your Perspective

As I mentioned earlier, you don't have much control over a lot of things in life, such as exactly when your house is going to sell or how the economy is doing. But you do have complete control over your perspective on these things. You can look at any situation and choose to focus on the good news as easily as the bad. This is a tremendous power that we all have.

The big trick is to be aware that you're operating under a particular perspective and that it colors everything you do. If you find you're not satisfied with the way you perceive your circumstances, you have the liberty to change that. And in so doing, you can create new, positive ways to deal with the situation, which is a form of control that can change everything.

▪ Count Your Blessings Every Day

When you're on the lookout for good things in your life, you automatically reduce the amount of time that you can focus on the negative. That's because it's nearly impossible to focus on both the positive and the negative simultaneously.

One simple way to draw your attention to the positive aspects of your life is by keeping a spiral notebook and listing at least 10 good things that happen everyday, no matter how small. Everywhere you look you'll find these little blessings: your five-year-old brought you a flower, you met a nice lady in line at the post office, you bought some amazingly juicy peaches, or you were able to pay your electric bill on time.

By making it a habit to list these blessings, it forces you to be on the lookout for them everywhere you go. This simple act is huge! As corny as this exercise may sound, it changes lives.

It also has a side benefit. If you feel happier, it can make your home environment feel more joyous. And, this subtle shift can actually attract a buyer who senses your "happy home vibes." Many people say they can feel the emotional energy in a house. They can tell if a place has a lot of heavy or sad energy, and they can tell if a place has happy occupants.

Which energy would you rather have around you? That's why you should seriously consider doing this exercise. It just might help you sell your house, and it definitely will make you feel better in the process.

■ Make Progress and Improvement

One way to shake the blues, no matter where they come from, is to make progress in some area of your life. Learning new skills and getting better at something is a salve that heals many wounds. The brain likes to have little victories.

So while your house is on the market, decide on a skill you'd like to learn or improve upon. It could be learning to speak a foreign language, playing an instrument, making jewelry or baking peach pies. There are hundreds of things you can get better at week after week, allowing you to watch your progress and feel a sense of growing achievement. You might even find something that you can make into a side business to earn extra income.

In addition, making progress is a great way to counteract stress and it gives you something to look forward to on a continuing basis. And then, when your property does sell, the progress that you've made gets to come with you wherever you go. Your time has not been wasted.

■ Take a Break and Reward Yourself

You'll like this one. Remember to reward yourself for all of your efforts in getting your house ready to show and keeping it that way. For example, promise yourself an hour in a hammock with a good book in exchange for spending your Saturday morning cleaning out part of the garage. It makes it a lot easier to be self-driven when you know there is something enjoyable waiting for you at the end of your chores.

By creating a work-reward system, you actually get four benefits at once. First, you motivate yourself to do the work in the first place. Second, you improve the chance of selling your house by doing the work. Third, you get to savor the reward when you're done with your chores. And fourth, you feel you've really earned whatever it is you've promised yourself.

If you had just crawled into your hammock knowing you've got a big mess in your garage, you'd probably feel a little guilty. (Especially if someone has been asking you to clean it!) But, if you know you've actually earned that hammock time, you'll feel much more self-righteous.

At least once a month while your house is on the market, you should also take a little time to do something enjoyable. Go to a matinee or an art show, or go on a picnic or a camping trip. Get creative. Bring a friend with you and have some well-deserved fun. Then, when you look back at the time when your house was on the market, you'll remember having some good times, instead of just cleaning and worrying.

▪ Use Your Sense of Humor

When you're stressed out or frustrated for an extended period of time, your sense of humor can slip away. Life just doesn't seem very funny anymore. Laughter, however, is exactly what you need when you're feeling anxious or down. It instantly lightens your heart and resets your mood. But how do you make yourself laugh when things don't seem too funny?

There are a lot of humor helpers that can get you started:

- **Read a funny book:** Do you have an author who makes you laugh? Dave Barry and travel writer Tim Cahill do it for me. My husband always knows when I am reading one of their books because I'm usually shaking the bed in laughing fits as I read late at night. It's amazing how quickly a few pages can adjust a bad mood. Suddenly things just don't seem so bad. Even if you don't feel like reading you should give it a try.

- **Watch something funny:** Rent a comedy, watch old funny syndicated TV shows or find something to laugh at on YouTube. I promise you'll feel much better. Sometimes watching old sitcoms such as *Seinfeld* or *I Love Lucy* is the best medicine when you're feeling blue. Not only will you find yourself laughing again, you'll be taking a relaxing break from worrying.

- **Talk to funny friends:** It's amazing how a friend can turn your spirits around, even if you're both complaining. Sometimes a mutual gripe session is the perfect thing. My friend and I like to play this game we call "Complaint Queen for a Day" where we both compete for who can do the best job of complaining. The winner gets to wear the imaginary Crown of Awfulness until the next time we play. Somehow just sharing our complaints makes us both feel better and we often find ourselves laughing at our own misery. If you know someone else who is suffering from the Home Seller's Blues at the same time you are, he or she could be your perfect complaint partner!

- **Play humorous games:** There are some funny games, such as Pictionary and Balderdash, that are almost guaranteed to make you laugh. In Pictionary, you can't help but chuckle at the ridiculous pictures most people draw. In Balderdash, everyone gets childishly creative making up new meanings for strange words. So if you want a happy distraction, pop some popcorn and sit down with a few friends for a game. Before you know it, you'll all be having a surprisingly good time.

- **Join a laughter club:** If you haven't heard of these clubs, don't laugh, they're actually real. And their sole purpose is to get people laughing. The first of such clubs appeared around 1995, when people gathered together on the streets in India just to share some laughter and lighten their spirits. The idea then spread around the world and now there are laughter clubs everywhere. There are even Certified Laughter Leaders who've made it their career to get people laughing! To find out more about these groups or to see if there is one in your area, just do a search on "laughter clubs" on the Internet.

- **Take an Improvisation Class:** This may sound scary but it really isn't bad at all. Even if you are a shy person you can do this because these classes usually get a whole group of people up and learning "improv" at the same time. You are not standing on a stage alone. (Unless you really want to!) And it's amazing what funny things come out of people's mouths when they don't know what they are going to say next. By the time your first class session ends, don't be surprised if your face muscles hurt from smiling.

As you can see, there are possibilities for finding laughter everywhere, but you do need to seek them out. As you know, laughter doesn't come knocking on your front door when you've got the Home Seller's Blues.

■ Move That Body!

Of course, I'd have to mention this one. Physical exercise is part of any program of maintaining your health and well-being. It gives you energy, elevates your mood, makes you sleep better and keeps chairs from collapsing under your weight. Even if you don't feel like exercising, get yourself moving anyway. Walk, hike, dance, jog, swim, or sweep! You might find it hard to get motivated at first, but afterwards you'll be glad you did.

■ Eat Foods That Love You Back

Even though eating a box of cookies feels more nurturing than gnawing on carrot sticks, it won't feel that way after you've eaten it. When you're trying to sell your house, you've got enough to deal with, without adding extra weight to all of the other stuff you've got to move.

So get yourself in the habit of buying and enjoying foods that are better for you—but also fun. Have you tried jicama for example? It's a big brown vegetable tuber that looks like a cross between a giant radish and a potato, but tastes more like a delicious, refreshing apple. Now there's a treat that won't make you feel guilty.

I also think those little bags of mini carrots are pretty good. They allow you to eat something crunchy and sweet, but won't make you feel sick or lethargic. And, if you accidentally eat a whole bag of carrots, you don't have to feel too guilty. But it's better not to eat a bag a day. I had a college roommate who did that and her palms and feet turned bright orange!

If you have to treat yourself to something sweet, buy it by the single serving instead of the larger size. That way you can't get too out of control. Then eat it slowly and savor it. Consider it a reward instead of a form of self-sabotage.

■ Stop Nighttime Panic Attacks

For some reason worries always seem bigger and badder when they strike in the middle of the night. A worry that seems the size of a little dog during the day can become the size of an elephant when you're surrounded by darkness. That's why it's important to have an arsenal of weapons to stop nighttime worries and panic attacks.

Here are five tried and true methods to quiet your nighttime mind. Start with one, and if you need more help, move on to the next. Or, you might find that using a combination of these will work the best for you.

You will also notice that I've left the most obvious sleep aid out—I don't mention chemical substances because that's a topic that goes far beyond this book. Plus, there are a lot of other ways to put yourself to sleep that don't have potential side effects on your body. Here is my top five natural sleep inducers:

1. Catch Yourself in the Act: The minute you realize that you're lying in bed worrying, take a deep breath and remind yourself that worries always seem scarier in the wee hours of the night or morning. That's just the way it is. During the light of day, troubles often shrink back down to normal proportions. Just knowing this can give you a certain degree of comfort and will provide you with a helpful perspective.

If gently telling yourself this doesn't work, feel free to yell using words such as, "SHUT UP! I'M NOT GOING TO DO THIS TO MYSELF RIGHT NOW!" You might be surprised at how well this can work. But you do have to make it clear that you mean business and you simply aren't going to let yourself go on fretting in your bedding.

The reason it's important to stop this nighttime worrying right when it starts is because it can become a bad habit. If you get up at 3:00 a.m. two nights in a row, there's a good chance you'll do it again the third night, and then the fourth. The next thing you know you'll be defining yourself as an insomniac worryholic. So it's important to nip the nighttime worry habit in the bud the minute you see it forming. If you have already formed this habit you can break it by catching yourself and giving yourself a good talking to.

2. Distract Yourself: If you continue to grind away at your worrisome thoughts, even though you've told yourself to stop, then you need to exchange your current thoughts for more relaxing ones. This may sound obvious, but it's amazing how seldom people remember to do this.

The trick is to find something to think about that can take up a lot of time. One of my favorite distractions is to think back on a great vacation or a cross-country drive. I review every day of the trip in detail, remembering where I stayed, the places I visited, the people I met, and the restaurants I stopped at along the way. By the time I get to the fourth or fifth day of my trip, I am usually back to sleep.

If you don't have a big trip that you can review, or if you've already used this technique recently, you can play the "A through Z" game. Begin with the letter A, and start naming foods, or places, or animals that start with A. Then move on to B, and so forth. Or review the names of your past girlfriends, or boyfriends, or places you have worked or lived, or try to recall what you did on your last ten birthdays.

An accountant once told me that she short circuits her midnight worries by boring herself back to sleep. She imagines herself going through column after column of numbers in a financial spreadsheet until she drifts away. Perhaps you too can find something really boring to think about to distract you from your more worrisome thoughts!

3. Consider Your Luck: You may not realize it when you're tossing and turning, but it's actually a pretty nice thing to be able to lie back in a safe warm bed and not have to do anything at all. There are a lot worse places you could be.

So, if you don't feel like focusing on any particular thought to distract yourself, you can simply think about how wonderful it is to curl up in bed for hours, surrounded by soft blankets and pillows and quietness. There is nothing you have to do but lie there and be comfortable. How many times have you wished you could do that in the middle of a chaotic, stressful day? Now is your chance and you don't have to feel the least bit guilty.

4. Move a Little: Sometimes you can get so caught up in a loop of reoccurring worries that your adrenaline starts pumping. In this case, you may need to get out of bed and move around a little to help calm down and break the worry loop.

Get up and have a drink of water, pace the hallway a couple of times, or take a trip to the bathroom and count the number of eyes you have. This might be just enough movement to disrupt your negative thought patterns so you can get back to sleep.

If you are still feeling agitated you might need to stay up a little longer. Get a cup of hot herbal tea, stretch a little, and force yourself to yawn. Yawns are contagious, even if they are your own! You might also choose to do a little reading. Pick something on the boring side, such as how to trim Coleus plants to encourage bushier foliage. For many people, after just a few pages they find their eyes closing and their restlessness fading away.

5. Write it Down: If none of the techniques above work, it's time to do something completely different. Take out some paper and write down what's bugging you. Yes, it's that journaling thing again. List everything that's on your mind, from your fears about global economic collapse to the possibility that pack rats are living in your crankcase. When you see it all there in front of you, it can feel oddly confirming and relieving. After you've written it all down, you're also likely to discover that you're getting sleepy. Now leave your worry list outside of the bedroom and go back to bed. Doing this has been the saving grace for me when I'm overwhelmed and nothing else helps. I don't use this technique first, but when I need it, it always works.

How to Take a Philosophical, Spiritual Approach to Home Selling Problems

Let's look at home selling difficulties from one last angle—and that's from more of a spiritual, big-picture viewpoint. Even if you aren't a believer in the unknown, unseen forces in the universe, you might still find comfort in considering a "bigger-picture" approach.

For example, the financial difficulties of not being able to sell your house can accidentally result in tapping into your hidden talents to create an extra income. Or, you might be learning that you have more patience and trust in life than you thought you had.

For me, being stuck with my house drove me to research and write this book. It not only stimulated my creativity and sent me in search of answers; it resulted in collecting information that I could share with others who had the same problem.

Here are a number of tips for taking a more spiritual approach to your home selling situation:

■ Could It Be It Isn't Time For You To Sell Your House Yet?

Maybe there's some reason you need to stay where you are a while longer. Long ago when I was having difficulty selling my San Francisco condo, I decided to take it off the market for several months. I had planned to move out of the city, but because it didn't sell I was stuck where I was. During that time, I met my husband. Had I sold my condo and moved away, I probably would never have met him. This did make me wonder, was my home selling difficulty "meant to be?"

Another young family I know was trying to sell their house for almost a year. They wanted to move to a new city but had not figured out the perfect place yet, so they spent their vacation times looking. Meanwhile they put their house on the market. It was a great house, ideally located, and attractively priced. No one could figure out why it wasn't selling though. Many potential buyers fell in love, but all of them ultimately decided against it.

Finally, the perfect buyers showed up—a young couple with a baby boy. The minute they walked into the house, they knew the house was made for them. Everything they wanted was there: a powder-blue children's room, a big dining room for family gatherings and a built-in workshop for dad.

What was amazing though was that this house-hunting couple decided to wait about a year before they started looking. They were expecting a child and they both were hoping to get job promotions so they could afford a nicer place. When the baby arrived and their job promotions came through, they went looking for their dream house and found it. The moment they walked through the front door and met the sellers, both couples had the odd feeling that it was meant to be.

It turned out to be perfect timing for the sellers as well. After a year of looking for a new city they finally found a place where they were excited to relocate. It seemed that both the buyers and sellers had to wait a year to get what they really wanted.

There are a lot of mysterious reasons why you could be stuck where you are. Once your home sells, you might realize the reason why. It just might be a matter of timing for either you, the buyer of your home, or both.

■ This Too Shall Pass

"This too shall pass." These four words can help you keep your sanity no matter how difficult your situation may seem. If you look at a history book of all the struggles and wars this world has been through, from the Peloponnesian wars to the Irish Potato Famine, these challenges all eventually pass.

One day, you too will look back and not feel the sting of the Home Seller's Blues. Just as you may have survived a bullying kid who used to chase you after school, a heartbreaking relationship, or a blabbermouth co-worker who made it difficult to get your work done, remember: this too shall pass.

■ There Are Two of You

At any given time, you can observe yourself and notice that you are actually two different people. One person is wise and understanding, who looks at things from a bigger perspective and feels there may be a reason for everything. This is your higher self. The other is the upset, worried person who stuffs big brownies in your mouth and feels that the world is trying to do you in. This is your lower self.

The important thing to realize is that one of you has the upper hand at any given time. The more you're aware of this, the more you can control which person is in the driver's seat, and know when to switch drivers.

When you find yourself operating from your lower self—stop, take a deep breath, recognize that you're currently experiencing the thought patterns and behaviors of your lower self, and gently acknowledge this keen observation. Then let the higher self do the driving for a while. This higher self will recognize there are answers out there, even if you haven't found them yet, and be open to creative possibilities.

If you need help accessing your higher self, take a quiet solo walk or get out in nature and listen carefully for the answers. All of us have access to this inner wise person. We just have to be aware that he or she is there for us when we need it.

■ See Yourself Moving

Try this exercise: stand at your front door (with the door open) and symbolically beckon the new owners to come forth. Imagine them walking up your driveway for the first time, looking very excited, because they know they've found their perfect new home.

Even though you can't physically see these people, it's good to know that they are out there and you are drawing them in. Now imagine these new buyers walking from room to room nodding in approval while discussing where they're going to place their furniture.

See yourself packing boxes with a smile on your face, knowing you've sold your home and you're about to embark on your next life chapter. Now imagine the paperwork for the sale being signed and stacks of boxes moving out of your house.

Hold these visions in your mind daily and don't give up on them, even if it takes a long time before it finally happens. The clearer and more often you envision what you want, the more it seems you help create a clear path for it to happen. Does it work? No one knows for sure, but it feels better than not doing it.

After all, every invention and dream the human race has ever achieved, started with our ability to see it in our mind's eye first. Man didn't spontaneously go to the moon. A lot of people spent time visualizing it into reality first.

Even if it feels as if you've got a better chance of going to the moon than selling your property, keep on imagining the entire moving process, from the buyer walking up to your door for the first time, to locking your door for the last time. It can't hurt. It also won't hurt to keep your house clean and drop the price if you need to!

■ Thank Your Home and Make it Clear You Are Ready to Move On

Make it clear to yourself and the world around you that you're ready to move on. When your intentions are not completely clear to you, it's harder to get what you want. Somehow your life gets tangled up and you don't know exactly why.

For example: you decide you want to move but you have mixed feelings. You don't want to leave your friends who live close by, and you don't know whether you'll like the new area where you plan to move. So even though your intent seems to be that you want to move, your intention isn't 100% pure. Maybe it's only about 70% pure.

As a result, subtle things can get in your way, such as you don't take perfect care of your house before showings. Perhaps you clean it only about 70% of the way. Or, maybe you don't want to reduce your property price by the amount your real estate agent suggests that you should. So you only reduce it 70% of that amount. These are just examples, but take a look at this in your own situation. Do you have some ambivalence about moving?

Metaphysical practitioners believe that the universe takes

you up on your ambivalent and confusing feelings, drawing toward you ambivalent results. For example, you end up attracting prospects who "kind of" want to buy your house, but aren't 100% sure, so they never make you a serious offer. That's why you need to make it clear to yourself that you are ready to move on—if you really are.

To help reinforce your sense of readiness to move on, take a few moments to honor and thank your property for all that it has meant to you. See your time of ownership as completed. Imagine symbolically untangling your emotional roots of connectedness from your house and lifting them out from underneath it. On some level this may also help potential buyers form a stronger attachment to your home, instead of feeling as if it's still deeply connected to you.

Even if you aren't a believer in metaphysics, the more you make it clear to yourself that you're ready to move on, the more you'll do what it takes to make it happen.

■ Employ Saint Joseph

Last but not least, even if you're not Catholic, you can always bury a small plastic statue of Saint Joseph, the Patron Saint of family, household needs and real estate transactions in your front yard. The roots of this tradition span hundreds of years back to Europe when a special sect of Catholic Sisters were said to bury their St. Joseph medals in the ground to help them secure more land for their convents.

Nowadays a special sect of home sellers believe that if you bury a statue of St. Joseph upside down facing the street, it will help you sell your property more quickly. Being no fool myself, I ran out and bought one of these statues and buried it outside the first house I had trouble selling.

It took a while for my home to sell, but it worked. Perhaps the sale had something to do with lowering my property price, making my house thoroughly inviting inside and out, and keeping everything wonderfully clean. But hey, it might have also been that statue. So I tried it again when I had trouble selling another house during the crash of 2007, and lo and behold it worked again.

Coincidence? Of course it might be. But when you want to feel in control of an uncontrollable situation, this might make you feel better. At least it feels as if you're taking some sort of action. (And I do have friends that wouldn't try selling a house without one.)

Where do you find these statues? The first place to look is on the Internet. You can find them on eBay, or in many other online stores. They often come in "St. Joseph Home Selling Kits," which include a history of the use of the statue, instructions for proper burial, a prayer to say while burying it, and the statue itself. Even if you don't have a front yard, you can still put your St. Joseph statue in an indoor houseplant near your front door.

A Short Story About Short Sales

Let's say you did everything right: after careful consideration you bought a nice house and you had enough money to pay your monthly bills. But then one day you discover you need to relocate for your work, or you get slammed with whopping medical bills or you lose your job. Uh-oh, suddenly you need to sell your home—and unfortunately your home value is now lower than the mortgage you owe. In other words, you're underwater.

Many people have found themselves in this situation, and

as a result, home sellers have turned to short sales as a means of getting out of financial trouble. In a short sale, you negotiate with your lender or lenders to sell your home for less than the full amount of mortgage you owe. A short sale, however, is not a simple way to get out of an investment gone wrong. You must truly be in a position of hardship.

I talked with Frank Joseph, the owner of Residential Realtors Northwest LLC, a real estate firm that specializes in short sales, for advice on what a short sale entails and how it can benefits sellers. Frank, who has helped many home owners through the short sale process, told me some good news:

First, your credit rating may not be as tarnished if you go through a short sale, versus a foreclosure. If you go through a foreclosure, you'll have to wait many years (often seven) before you can purchase another home. But if you go through a short sale, you may be able to purchase another home in 12 to 36 months, depending upon any debt you owe.

Another thing that worries short-selling home sellers is whether they'll have to dig into their 401K retirement funds to pay off their loan. Frank told me this is not usually the case and there's a good chance a home seller's 401K will not be affected.

However, there are often tax implications as a result of a short sale, so it's important to speak to an accountant or attorney to understand the potential impact it can have on your future finances.

In terms of the best advice for proceeding with a short sale, Frank recommends selecting a Realtor with experience in handling short sales and in negotiating with the various parties involved. A short sale transaction will also flow easier and faster if you can quickly provide all of the documents necessary, which include a hardship letter explaining your circumstances, past bank statements and tax returns, pay stubs, a financial statement, utility bills, home owner association information (if applicable), and any other documents requested by lenders.

Because short selling is a complex, continually evolving topic, your best bet is to talk personally with a Realtor experienced in the field. I just wanted to give you some basics, in case a short sale scenario is in your future.

In Case Of Foreclosure

I'd be remiss if I didn't discuss foreclosure in this book, with so much of it going on all around us. Although my goal is to help you sell your home and cope with the selling process before you reach a foreclosure (or short sale) situation, it's important to address how to cope with it in case it does happen.

I've had a number of close friends and acquaintances go through foreclosure, and although I haven't experienced it myself, I have been on the unfortunate end of a massive bank fraud case. So I know what it's like to suddenly have a major chunk of one's financial worth suddenly disappear, and the life-changing impact it can have both in the present and in the future.

It's shocking, numbing, nauseating and overwhelming, and you probably feel it's profoundly unfair, or you're kicking yourself for past decisions made—or you're experiencing both feelings simultaneously. As a friend of mine said, "I felt like throwing up on my doorstep." However, if the fear of foreclosure has been looming over you for a long time, after it's behind you, you might feel as if a wrecking-ball of anguish has been lifted off your shoulders. If there's nothing more you can do about it, you can finally put down that heavy weight you've been carrying around for months.

After the initial shock fades away you begin to realize you're still the same person you were before, even though your pride may be temporarily damaged. You understand that you are not your house, and you discover that many good things in life still exist. You can still enjoy a great cup of coffee, hear the birds sing, spend time in nature, stare at the stars, have a good laugh with family or friends, have a rousing conversation with your pet, dive into a good book, listen to great music—the list is pretty endless. The old pleasures are still very much alive.

I participated in a study once where we were asked what we'd do on a daily basis if we won the lottery. Surprisingly, many of the things on our lists involved activities that required little or no money. Many items had more to do with a *frame of mind* that emphasized enjoying life more and striving to be our best selves. For example, participants wrote they would exercise more, do volunteer work, delve into creative art and writing projects, grow a garden, cook healthier meals, get out in nature frequently and spend quality time with family and friends.

Outside of the obvious lottery dreams of traveling around the world, buying a Ferrari and purchasing a villa in Italy, most of the daily activities were things that somebody who just went through a foreclosure (or a massive bank fraud) could do as well. It's just a matter of identifying what these enjoyable things are, and making time to do them. This might mean minimizing the hours spent on "time-killing" activities such as hanging out online continuously, watching TV, or being around people you don't really enjoy.

You may also find that once the initial shock is over, your friends are surprised at how well you cope with your loss. It's human nature to proceed onward, taking one step after another, instead of permanently crumpling up in a ball. I just talked to one friend who faced foreclosure recently. She was enthusiastically telling me about a new client she had found, and how she now had room for a large home office in her new rental house.

After our own financial loss, I remember a friend staring at me in awe. She'd never met anyone personally who had gone through such a thing and she was amazed I was still able to eat and drink and talk and breathe. It actually amazed me too. Here this horrible thing had just happened, and I wasn't dwelling on it non-stop—I was busy getting my life back in order. In this way, I think our ability as humans to adapt to situations and cope is just incredible. It's natural for us to start tapping into our inner and outer resources, much of which we may not have even known we had.

Economist and author Albert O. Hirschman had a theory he called the "Hiding Hand Principle." In essence, his idea was that hidden in our future are the negative events we will eventually face. But also hidden, on the other side of the "hiding hand," are the resources, opportunities, coincidences, events and people who'll be there to help us tackle our problems when they arise.

I've seen this principle in action amongst my foreclosed friends. One ended up moving in with her boyfriend, a professional French chef with a gorgeous apartment, who made her killer chocolate mousse any time she demanded it. She described her life as being far better than it was during the agonizing months that led up to losing her home. Another acquaintance moved in with her newly divorced daughter and grandchildren. This living arrangement proved to be a gift to them all, giving the whole family much needed time together to heal from their losses.

Of course, no one wants to experience these negative events, but it's important to know that as the "Hiding Hand Principle" states and as our own human nature suggests: not only do we have the mechanisms to cope with what we face, life on the other side of a disaster can provide us with new and desirable opportunities, if we are open to looking for them.

CHAPTER TEN

How To Get More People To Your Front Door

It all boils down to being a numbers game. The more potential buyers you lure into your house, the greater the probability of finding someone who will make you an offer. The way to do this is through creative, targeted marketing.

This means doing much more than putting a sign on your lawn and listing your house on the Multiple Listing Service, although these are clearly important. To get to the widest audience of potential buyers possible, you need to think both inside and outside of the box. Fortunately, there are many things you can do yourself, even if you're working with a real estate agent. By taking personal action, you'll also feel a sense of control over the situation.

Here are a number of savvy steps you can take to help sell your property:

■ Pick a Great Real Estate Agent

If you're planning on using an agent, it's important to do your homework and choose one who will work hard on your behalf.

Before you hire Jane Smith, your friendly next-door neighbor and Realtor, find out the answers to these questions:

- **Is the agent successfully selling homes during the current market conditions?** Do you know any prior sellers who used Jane as their agent, who can tell you about their experience working with her?

- **Does the agent provide you with up-to-date, realistic pricing information?** Some agents may tell you to list your home for a high selling price just to get your listing. Even though a higher price may sound appealing, it's not necessarily in your best interest. That's why it's important to pick an agent who'll give you detailed information about the other homes on the market in your area and recent sales activity and trends, and then, based on this data, determine a realistic asking price for your home.

- **Does the agent have a solid long-term marketing plan?** Find out how the agent plans to target and promote your home to buyers and other agents. Does she have a comprehensive Internet marketing strategy to ensure your home gets maximum online exposure? Will she promote your home through a variety of methods? Will she be holding open houses?

- **Does the agent provide you with suggestions on how to enhance the visual appeal of your home?** Good agents will (politely) let you know if you need to remove excess clutter, and will give you ideas for presenting your home in its best light. She may also provide you with a list of experts who can help you repair or enhance your property, including names and numbers of handymen, painters, stagers and gardeners.

- **How accessible is the agent?** Can you reach Jane easily by phone, email, text or through extra sensory perception? Does she return messages in a reasonable amount of time? This is important because if you have a hard time reaching your agent, so will house hunters and their agents. A good Realtor will also keep in contact with you to let you know what's going on and the progress being made—even if it's slow.

- **How many photos will the agent be posting online?** Will she post the maximum amount the MLS allows or will she post beyond this number on her own site—to get even more exposure for your home? The more attractive visual information you can provide potential buyers, the more likely your property will be remembered and visited.

- **Will the agent create a highlight sheet detailing the features and benefits of your area?** (And, is the agent savvy about the amenities in your area?) It used to be you only needed to describe the features of your home, but now with the increased inventory of houses on the market, you also need to post and promote what's unique about your particular neighborhood. (You'll be reading more about this later in this chapter.)

- **Do other people *like* your agent?** This may sound strange, but I've heard of people who've had trouble getting buyers to see their homes because they discover that other agents don't like working with the seller's agent! Buyer's agents know that they'll have to negotiate with your difficult agent if their clients want to make an offer, so they may be less likely to point out your home in the first place. In a hot housing market this isn't an issue, because every property is a precious commodity. However, when there is a high inventory of properties to pick from, you don't need any additional obstacles to attracting buyers.

■ Get The Agent Advantage

You may be thinking about selling your home on your own because there's something nice about not having to pay commissions to real estate agents. You can either pocket that money yourself or lower your home price by the amount you would otherwise pay in commissions—which may attract more buyers. This can work if you have real estate experience, marketing and negotiation skills, and a knowledgeable attorney by your side. But for most sellers, the for-sale-by-owner (FSBO) experience can be tough going, especially in a slow-moving housing market.

As much as I like figuring out ways to do things inexpensively, which I've emphasized throughout this book, I've learned that it pays to call on experts in the fields where I lack knowledge. That's why I've finally given up cutting my own hair. Even though I have decades of experience using scissors, and "self-styling" saves me a lot of time, money and mileage, I almost always end up upset and embarrassed.

That's why I prefer using real estate agents when it comes to selling my own property. They've got the expertise, systems and networks in place that most home sellers lack. I find that if you pick a good agent from the start (using the criteria in the previous section), you'll have a number of advantages over trying to sell it on your own.

Here is what a good agent brings to the table:
• Many house hunters are leery of FSBO houses. They often

feel safer when they see a "For Sale" sign representing a well-known agency. In a buyer's mind, these traditional signs signify that an experienced third-party agent has viewed the property, given it a stamp of approval, and will be highly involved in the negotiation and transaction process. When house hunters see a store-bought "For Sale" sign, they don't know what they'll find inside the door, whether the home has major flaws the owner is trying to hide, or whether they'll walk in on a potentially difficult or dangerous person. All of this can equate to fewer potential visitors—especially during slow times when there are fewer buyers and an already high inventory of homes on the market, represented by recognized agencies.

- Buyer's agents are more likely to point out homes listed by known real estate agencies because they have ready-access to detailed information about these properties. In addition, they often preview these places on their own first, and then bring any number of clients over to see it. This means more potential visits from a higher volume of agents, each representing their own stock of clients.

- The house hunters that come through recognized real estate agencies are usually more traditional themselves. They are often vetted in advance and pre-qualified for a loan, which means you're less likely to have visits from "looky-loos" who can't afford your house. When selling on your own, anyone can call you up directly and ask for a tour—which can even be dangerous—if you find yourself alone with the wrong person.

- There is more work involved in the home selling process than meets the eye. Some sellers believe all you need to do is shoot some attractive photos, put a sign in front of your house, list it on major home selling websites, then sign the papers when an offer comes in. But today, with pickier buyers and more regulations, the entire process is trickier. Real estate offices have effective systems in place to deal with these difficulties. They have extensive marketing networks and strategies, practiced negotiation skills that can keep nervous buyers from walking away during the sales process, and often, a pool of cost-effective repair people you can hire to fix home problems. In addition, experienced agents are aware of regulatory changes: from how appraisals are handled, to changes in the required paperwork. They also act as a buffer, answering phone calls, dealing with house hunter questions and following up with potential buyers, so sellers can go on with their own lives.

- Agents can take you to see comparable properties in your area so you are more comfortable with the asking price they recommend. Buyers are extremely price sensitive when the economy slows, and if they're working with their own agent, they know exactly how much house they can get for their money. If you're selling your home on your own and choosing a price based on what feels right to you, you may be asking too much, or too little, which doesn't serve you either way.

- Agents often have a wide network of contacts, both locally and possibly nationally and internationally (if they're working with relocation services and overseas offices). It's an agent's job to schmooze, so they're often members of local and national associations where they're in constant contact with others. Realtors who are part of a bigger office also share information with co-workers, so their marketing efforts are multiplied by a team of people. Agents also attract buyers through their own paid advertising, including magazine, newspaper and online promotions. In addition, if an agent has an office in a high-traffic pedestrian area, they can post flyers in their windows where house hunters will see them.

- Because experienced agents are familiar with the legal ramifications of selling property in a particular state or country, they can keep you from getting involved in a legal battle over mistakes made when filling out paperwork. This is one headache you don't need!

- Real estate transactions can be overwhelming, especially if you're busy working, or going through a rocky time in your life. I've had real estate agents come to my aid in many unexpected ways: from finding me the exact match of paint to touch up the exterior of my house, to bringing me homemade chicken soup when I was sick!

My final piece of advice on Realtors is to find one you like and stick with him or her. Out of desperation, many sellers keep switching agents, hoping it will help them sell their house faster. If your agent isn't putting forth the effort, moving on is understandable, but if the problem is a slow economy with few buyers, changing agents won't make much difference. It's like trying out different makes of cars to get ahead during daily rush hour traffic. You can switch from a reliable Honda, to a fast Porsche, to a luxurious Cadillac, and still be stuck in the same slow-moving conditions. I learned this myself after switching agents and realizing, after the fact, that it had nothing to do with who represented me. There just weren't many buyers out there, so "changing vehicles" didn't help me any.

In fact, it can actually end up hurting a seller if you gain a reputation for constantly switching agents. Since agents put up their own advertising money and don't get paid until they make a sale, they may be concerned about investing in a property if they think the seller is going to drop them on their heads in a couple of months—as the seller may have already demonstrated with a slew of other agents.

■ Employ Niche Marketing

Is there something special about your house that will attract a particular group of people? If your home has a unique feature such as a large RV garage, horse stable, dog run, workshop, artist studio, or a vegetable garden, you may have something that will appeal to a particular group of buyers.

If your home is adjacent to a desirable location, such as an area known for windsurfing, golfing, fishing, sailing, organic farming, or if you're located in a college town, high-growth business area or retirement hot spot, you also have a built-in niche of potentially interested buyers.

Once you've discovered who would be interested in your property or area, the next step is to figure out how to market to this group of people. For example, if your home has horse stables, you might consider advertising in equestrian magazines or websites. Or, create a blog geared to this niche market and include in some of your posts that your property is for sale. (You can also include as many home photos as you want—it's your blog!) You may just find an equestrian reader who happens to be looking for a property that's perfect for horses.

If your home is next to a bus or rail line that enables residents to easily commute to a major urban area, your property would appeal to many working professionals. You can market to them by advertising in newspapers and local magazines that commuting professionals read. Or, you can post your information online and place flyers where these people congregate during lunch hour, over the weekend, or at gyms and local golf courses. Make sure though, that your information states that your home is within easy walking distance to public transportation to get the attention of this particular group.

Then there's an entirely different way to look at niche marketing: in some odd cases you may be able to attract a specific pool of buyers because of *who* has lived in your home, past or present. For example, one clever young woman advertised her condo as a "Good Luck" condo, because everyone who had lived there ended up finding their husbands-to-be. Her creative niche marketing paid off. Soon after she began advertising, a woman bought her place because she too was hoping for a lucky break in the love department. Had the seller not advertised in this way, her condo would never have grabbed the attention of the woman who bought it.

If by chance anyone famous has ever lived in your house, this would also attract a particular group of people. One homeowner in San Francisco knew for a fact that Jerry Garcia of the Grateful Dead had once lived in his upstairs bedroom. The owner included this in his advertising, and not surprisingly, sold the home to a long-time Grateful Dead fan. Famous musicians, artists, sports celebrities, chefs, movie stars and well-known business founders have all had to live somewhere. If by chance they lived in your house, even in their humble beginnings, you may have an unusual niche market of buyers.

■ Spread The Word Throughout Your Community

Another easy way to get the word out locally is to hang flyers anywhere they'd get noticed: in your city's library or community center, in grocery and convenience stores, at restaurants, coffee houses and gyms, and in any other high-traffic place where you can lawfully post flyers.

You never know if someone in your area is looking to upsize, downsize, or move from a rental, but stay close by. Your flyer might be just the motivation they need to take the first step. This is also a cheap, fast way to stand out from the crowd of ads in the newspaper and online, especially if your flyer features nice pictures of your home and lists its most attractive features.

■ Alert Your Neighbors

Many times people don't think about promoting their homes to their neighbors because they think, "They already have a house." But these neighbors might have family members, friends, or co-workers who might be interested in moving to your area.

By providing your neighbors with sales flyers and asking if they know of anyone who might be interested, you can get some attention from people who would not have found out about your place otherwise. Your neighbors could also serve as your allies by pushing their friends or family members to buy your house because they want them to live close by.

I've actually seen this work firsthand. When my neighbors were trying to sell their house, they gave their sales flyer to a couple who were building a house down the street. This couple sent the flyer to their good friends out of state to tempt them to relocate next to them. The out-of-state couple flew out, looked at the house and bought it. All it took was alerting the neighbors by giving them a flyer!

■ Hold Open Houses (And why you should do it)

Some people love them, some people hate them. And that goes both for sellers and real estate agents. I've heard some agents say that open houses don't do anything except stress out the owners and waste an agent's time.

But I also know that some very successful agents think that open houses are a great way to capture sales. Here is their reasoning: homebuyers often spend much of their time and energy looking at houses even when their agent isn't around. They look at web sites, newspapers, local real estate magazines, and they go to open houses. Some agents urge their clients to go out and see as many open houses as they can, and then report back if they find anything they would be interested in buying. Since real estate agents can only show their clients so many houses in a day, this allows their clients to cover more ground and thus, increase the odds of finding a home they would like to buy.

In addition, the more houses that are on the market, the less chance there is for agents to potentially show your house. So by holding your house open, you increase the odds of a buyer accidentally wandering through your front door and falling in love. In fact, many times people fall for houses that don't even match the description of what they were originally looking for. But once they see a house they love, they decide to buy it anyway.

This actually happens all the time. People tell their agent they want a two-bedroom place, but then they fall in love with a three-bedroom home during an open house. Or, they say they want to spend $250,000, but proceed to fall for a $300,000 house that they visit during an open house. So it pays to attract a wider audience of potential buyers than those who are just looking for the specific qualifications of your house.

The fact that many sellers and agents don't like open houses is something to use to your advantage. The fewer open houses there are, the more yours will stand out! So while other home sellers keep their doors closed, you can hold yours open and grab more attention.

Now, I know it's a hassle to hold an open house and you might be afraid that the only people who will attend are your nosy neighbors, but it may be well worth it. Who cares if your neighbors come looking? Once you sell your house, you'll probably never see them again anyway. Besides, if they like it, maybe they'll tell others about it.

Then there's the concern over having your belongings stolen. To reduce this concern, you should remove anything valuable, hide medications that are in your bathroom medicine cabinet, and put away anything that is easy to take that has meaning to you.

If you follow my earlier advice to "depersonalize" your house and get rid of the clutter, this should eliminate much of the potential for pilfering. And who's to say you can't be home if you really want to be? It isn't a federal law punishable by five years of imprisonment if you're found at home during your open house.

Just pretend you're a paid plant-waterer, helper or a fellow house hunter. If you have a big house, you can also ask several friends to watch over various parts of your house so that visitors can't walk through your rooms alone.

Also realize that most people aren't there to steal your stuff.

How many open houses have you walked through where you didn't walk off with the seller's china and perfume? If you're like most people, you have never stolen anything during an open house and probably felt intrusive enough just touring a stranger's rooms.

■ Use the Right Words to Promote Your House

In a slow real estate market and in a slow economy people are often nervous about investing in a home. They want to know they are making a wise decision. They also want to feel that their home will be a source of comfort and peace in a scary, troubled world. That's why it's important to craft your words carefully to appeal to what motivates buyers in a slow market.

Because prospective buyers are looking for good investments, spell out all the reasons your home is a good financial choice.

Here are some ideas to get you started:

- Is your home priced below other comparable homes?
- Do you have energy efficient appliances or heating and cooling systems?
- Is your home well insulated?
- Is your property inexpensive to maintain?
- Are you close to public transportation or within walking distance to shops and services, enabling you to save money on gas and car expenses?
- Do you have the space available to grow a garden or do you presently have one?
- If you live in a condo or town house and pay monthly Home Owner's Association dues, are your dues lower than other nearby developments?

You also want your home description to appeal to a buyer's desire for comfort and enjoyment. The right words can stir positive emotions, which can make all the difference between whether a buyer chooses to tour your house or other houses on the market.

Here are some examples of comforting descriptions:
- A warm brick fireplace
- A built-in window seat for reading and relaxing
- A bright and sunny breakfast nook
- A dining room perfect for family dinners
- Beautiful views of old oak trees
- A babbling brook in your backyard
- A stone patio for enjoying your morning coffee
- Located next to an award-winning bakery

You get the picture. You want to create an image of a home that is easy for people to see themselves enjoying on a daily basis.

■ Create A Highlight Sheet

Many people who come to see your home won't know a lot about your neighborhood. Even though they might get a flyer that lists your home's best features inside and out, they might not know the advantages of your particular area or region.

For example, do you have a big park, pool, community center or award-winning golf course close by? Is your house in a choice school district? Do you have a good medical center or doctor's offices in the vicinity? Can you walk to the public library, the post office or a great grocery store from your house? Is there a community garden in your neighborhood? Does your area sponsor a lot of events? How many restaurants, bistros and coffee houses are close by? Do you have easy access to public transportation? Does your area have a low crime rate?

There are so many things you can add to a list like this. If you run low on ideas, ask friends and neighbors who live in (and love) your area. They might tell you things you haven't even thought about or have taken for granted.

For example, do you know if your county has a lower tax rate than other nearby counties? This can save you a lot of money. A friend of mine chose to buy a house in a particular county for this very reason. He has saved thousands because of it, including the tax on his new car! If you're in such an area, you'll want to promote this fact to potential buyers.

Take all of this information, and put it on a highlight sheet to distribute along with your flyer and on websites. Include your address, MLS number and contact information so a buyer can easily find you.

It might just be that your highlight sheet acts as a tie-breaker in the case that a buyer is trying to decide between several houses. At the very least, it will make your home remembered.

▪ Create Your Own Email Marketing Campaign

One very easy way to pass your home information on to others is to do your own email promotional campaign. Even if you're working with a real estate agent, it doesn't hurt to spread your information out as far and wide as possible through the use of email contacts.

In your email promotion, list all the tasty features and

information about your property, including photos and information from your area highlight sheet. Also include a catchy subject line and a heading to increase the odds that your message will be opened and read. Then email it to your friends, family members and associates with instructions to pass it on to others who may be interested. Before you know it, your email might attract a buyer from far away.

My friend did this and found a buyer for her home in just a couple of weeks. For her, it was a fast, easy, inexpensive form of advertising that paid off big time.

▪ Put Yourself Online All the Time

Make sure your home is listed on as many online sites as possible. For example, you can list your home on http://www.craigslist.org, http://www.zillow.com, http://www.trulia.com, http://www.realestate.yahoo.com, Google classifieds and many local websites in your particular area. The more exposure you get, the greater your chances are of finding interested prospects. And the beauty of Internet marketing is that the whole world can discover your house with very little effort on your part.

▪ Take Advantage of Social Media Tools

Spread the word about your property far, wide, fast and free using Internet networking tools such as Facebook, Twitter, YouTube, blogs and the many other tools which are emerging all the time. You can quickly and easily tell all your friends about your house on Facebook, post some great looking photos of it and offer a tasty finder's fee for anyone who connects you with a buyer. Do the same on Twitter and ask your friends to retweet the message to their friends. The opportunities using social media just continue to expand, so if you keep up with the latest tools you'll have multiple channels to help spread the word.

■ Create Your Own 30 to 60 Second Sales Pitch

There is always the chance that you're going to run into someone somewhere who may be interested in hearing about your house, either for themselves or to tell someone else about it. For example, you might be lunching with a table full of business people during a conference and you end up telling them that you're selling your house. They in turn ask for more information. This is when you need a short verbal sales pitch memorized and ready to go.

What you say can make all the difference in whether or not they want to investigate your home further. The more *visual* you make your pitch, the better.

Let me give you an example. You could quickly rattle off "The house has three bedrooms, two baths, a kitchen, and a backyard." Or, you could say, "The house has three spacious bedrooms filled with lots of natural light, beautiful views of the hills and two baths with spa shower heads and granite countertops. The kitchen has new knotty pine cabinetry and a sunny window seat, and the backyard has a rose garden, a built-in barbeque and a dining area." Which of these two descriptions do you think would motivate a house hunter to come over and take a look?

Remember to also describe your home in terms of the features that make it a good investment, as well as a comforting place to live in on a daily basis. As I mentioned earlier in this chapter, during a slow housing market when people are concerned about investing, the right description can help offset their fears.

If you're selling your home on your own and receiving phone calls from interested buyers, having a quick sales pitch is especially important. In fact, you should have a written script next to the phone, which describes your home's features in beautiful detail. It may not sound like much fun to write such a pitch, but that little extra effort might help bring in a buyer where you least expect it.

■ Offer Someone a Great Opportunity

Here's an idea that might work in certain situations and it's definitely thinking outside the box. Sarah Taylor, author of the legal guidebook, Pro Se Warrior, http://www.prosewarrior.com, shares what she did when she wanted to quickly sell a spec home she had built:

Rather than waiting for a buyer to approach her, she approached the wealthiest man in town who owned the local country club and golf course. Sarah told him that she would sell him her house for $50,000 below the appraised value if he would close escrow within 15 days. To make the deal sweeter she told him that he could sell the house to another party as long as Sarah was paid within 15 days. (For example, the country club owner could sell the house for $40,000 below the appraised value and make $10,000 on the transaction.)

The club owner took Sarah up on her offer and sold the house to one of his own employees in what Sarah called a "win-win" situation—the employee was able to buy the house at a great price, the country club owner made a profit on the sale, and Sarah sold the house and got her money in 15 days!

Now you might not be able to sell your home to the richest person in town, but there are some creative ideas in this. Maybe, for example, you can approach a company or organization that would be interested in purchasing your home (or condo or townhouse) at a very attractive price to lodge out-of-town employees or contractors on extended stays. This could be a "win" for companies, because they would no longer have to pay for expensive hotel nights and instead would own the property as part of their business.

The bottom line is to think of a particular person (or group) who would benefit from being targeted directly with a deal too good to pass up.

▪ Throw in a Gift with the Sale

Here's an idea that can work, depending on which marketing strategies are in favor when you're selling your home, and the current regulations in the real estate industry. Offering incentives to buyers can be an effective way to get your home noticed and remembered. However, incentives can fall out of favor for a variety of reasons, such as buyers preferring a rock-bottom home price over a free gift or service, too many sellers doing the same thing, or changes in lending or government regulations that make offering incentives more complicated. That's why it's important to get professional advice on the matter in your state (or country) before announcing your incentive to buyers. If you discover that this strategy is currently being used successfully and it's safe in terms of regulations, there's a world full of goodies you can offer to make your home stand out in a buyer's mind.

I recommended to one client that they throw in their huge screen television with the sale of their home. I suggested this because they were selling their home in an area where hundreds of similar homes were sitting on the market at the same time. If they wanted to stand out from all of the other reduced-price houses, they needed to do something different. (Besides, moving that colossal TV would have been a pain anyway.)

The sellers took me up on this idea. Within a month they sold their house to a single man who was a big sports fan. True, he could have purchased his own TV and maybe paid a little less for another house in the area, but he just couldn't resist someone throwing in a giant television for free. How often in life does anyone give you a great, big, free anything?

A car dealership owner can throw in a new car. Restaurant owners can offer a monthly dinner out. I heard about one seller who offered fresh-baked cookies delivered to the buyer's door each month. There are hundreds of ideas like this, even if you don't own a business or store of your own. You can still tell buyers you'll pay their closing costs, moving costs, give them a free gardener or a cleaning service for a year, or throw in a home warranty or a luxurious bed and breakfast weekend—any of which may give you a leg up on your competition.

▪ Offer a Rent-to-Own Deal

You might be able to attract an interested buyer who otherwise couldn't afford a down payment on your home by offering a rent-to-own arrangement. Here is how it works: the home seller agrees to rent the property to an interested buyer for a given period of time, such as 18 months, with the option to purchase the property for a specified price at the end of the rental period.

This buyer puts down an up-front, non-refundable payment

of a small percent of the homes value, for example 2%, which locks in an agreed-upon purchase price and goes toward the home's purchase. In addition, a certain portion of the buyer's monthly rent can also be credited toward the purchase price. The benefit of this is that at the end of the rental period, the renter has had time to save up for a larger down payment, and if necessary, improve a less than stellar credit rating to increase their chance of qualifying for a loan.

The positive side of lease-to-own deals for owners is that the renters tend to be very conscious about caring for the property as if it's their own, which they hope it may soon become. They will also be more likely to pay their monthly rent on time.

In markets with rising home prices, rent-to-own deals can be advantageous to renters who are able to lock in a lower sales price than if they waited 18 months before buying a house. In markets with falling home prices, however, the renter can get stuck paying a higher price than the house may be worth 18 months later. Of course, the renter can choose to walk away, but the owner (depending on the initial agreement) gets to keep the money that the renter initially put down at the start of the contract.

▪ Consider Swapping Houses

When times are tough, don't rule out highly creative opportunities. One innovative way that people are getting out from under their homes and into new places is by doing a home swap across the city, country, or even overseas. There are a number of websites, such as http://www.goswap.org or http://www.onlinehousetrading.com that help people interested in swapping houses find each other.

Both you and other interested swappers post information about your properties, such as size, location, price and other criteria, which is then placed in a database to find potential matches. The beauty of these swaps is that both parties do not have to own a home of equal value. One family may be looking to trade up to a bigger house while the other is looking to downsize. The difference in price is handled through mortgages and other secure, adult-like methods.

The home-swapping phenomenon is a world unto its own, and the best way to learn more about it is to go online and look at what is available. There you'll find houses all over the country, including photos and what the owners are looking for in exchange for their houses. It's really a pretty exciting trend and an interesting way to find a buyer in a slow real estate market.

SOME FINAL WORDS

Being stuck with a property when you want to move on is an unnatural state for any species. While other species can get up and crawl or fly away, we humans are stuck having to pay down a mortgage and wait until a new owner shows up.

Fortunately we have other forms of control:
- We can change our perception of the situation.
- We can figure out how to take advantage of our tough luck.
- We can change our environment to make it more appealing.
- We can attract niche groups of people to view our property.
- We can change our lives to make "staying put" more productive and enjoyable.
- We can throw in such things as purchase incentives.
- We can throw out things to make our living spaces less cluttered.
- And we can lower the price of our property when necessary.

Because we have this degree of control, the home selling period can accidentally be a great time in our lives. One of my all-time favorite quotes by Thomas Carlyle is:
> *"The block of granite*
> *which was an obstacle in the pathway of the weak*
> *becomes a stepping-stone in the pathway of the strong."*

As a result of having the Home Seller's Blues, you can discover inner resources, creativity, and talent you never knew you had. In fact, you could end up inadvertently changing your entire life for the better.

So, when moving day finally arrives and your property changes hands, remember to take a moment to be thankful for everything you've learned, thankful for the new owner coming along, and thankful for the new chapter that is about to open up to you.

Also, don't forget to do something special for yourself to mark the occasion. Open a fine bottle of wine, spend a day at the beach, or go out for a celebration dinner. You deserve it all the way!

REFERENCES & LINKS

Here are the websites and reference materials I've listed in this book in the order in which they make their appearance. I apologize in advance for any references or products that may no longer be available when you go looking for them. Unfortunately, I find it hard to make the world obey my wishes for permanent web addresses, links and products, and as a result some things may change without my permission. But hopefully, much of what you are looking for will be available or quickly found by conducting your own Internet searches.

INTRODUCTION
Audio Program: *Instant Guts! How To Take A Risk and Win in Every Area of Your Life* by Joan Gale Frank. Available for audio download on http://www.amazon.com

CHAPTER ONE (no references listed)

CHAPTER TWO (no references listed)

CHAPTER THREE
Artwork by Thomas McKnight (Master of creating images that look like beautifully staged home interiors and exteriors.) http://www.prints.com

Suppliers of Zeolite (Natural odor absorber for petrochemicals and other smells.)
http://www.allergystore.com/

CHAPTER FOUR
Painting Techniques
Book: *Paint Can! Techniques, Patterns, and Projects for Bringing Color into Every Room* by Sunny Goode, Sterling Publishing, 2006
Interior Typography (Stick-on letters and words to beautify your walls.) http://www.wonderfulgraffiti.com
Room Lighting (Full spectrum light bulbs to create "indoor sunshine.")
http://www.realgoods.com/
Light Switch Plates (Light switch plates of all kinds to fit every room in your home.)
http://www.switchhits.com
http://www.switchplategallery.com
Mobiles (Hanging mobiles in many styles and sizes.)
http://www.hangingmobilegallery.com
http://www.konrads.com

CHAPTER FIVE (no references listed)

CHAPTER SIX
Address Plaques (To beautify your home and let visitors know they've arrived at the correct address.)
http://www.addressplaqueshops.com
Mailboxes (Increase your home's curb appeal with an attractive mailbox.)
http://www.curbdecor.com
http://www.i-mailboxes.com/

http://www.mailboxworks.com
Stepping-Stone Making Kits (Kits and stones to lead the way to your door.)
http://www.milestonesporducts.com
http://www.yardlover.com
Outdoor Speakers (Bring your music outdoors with attractive speakers to fit your landscape.)
http://www.skymall.com
http://alloutdoorspeaker.com/
http://www.stereostone.com

CHAPTER SEVEN (no references listed)

CHAPTER EIGHT (no references listed)

CHAPTER NINE (no references listed)

CHAPTER TEN
Online Real Estate Marketing Sites (Spread the word about your home far and wide.)
http://www.Realtor.com
http://www.craigslist.org
http://www.zillow.com
http://www.trulia.com
http://www.realestate.yahoo.com
Book: *Pro Se Warrior,* http://www.prosewarrior.com, by Sarah Taylor, 2010. (A book about legal contracts and advice on many subjects from a savvy legal advocate.)
Home Swapping (Tired of being stuck in the same house? Exchange your home for someone else's.)
http://www.goswap.org
http://www.onlinehousetrading.com

About the Author

 Joan Gale Frank is a veteran real estate investor and award-winning writer/producer for video, audio and TV commercials. She has also served as a marketing writer for many Fortune 500 companies, including Apple Inc., Intel Corporation, and Johnson & Johnson.

Ms. Frank's audiobook, *Instant Guts!* a motivation program on how to take intelligent risks in every area of your life, was nominated by Audiophile as "Best Personal Growth Program of the Year" and featured in NPR's Wireless Catalog. She has appeared on numerous radio and TV interviews, and frequently speaks at business conferences. She holds a Master's Degree specializing in adult education and motivation, and a Master's Degree in Public Health from U.C.L.A.

In addition, Ms. Frank specializes in cooking pasta with a variety of sauces and will try practically anything available at Trader Joes.

Ms. Frank can be reached at joanf@homesellersblues.com
For print and ebook information and purchasing:
http://www.homesellersblues.com
Home Seller's Blues Blog: http://housesellingblues.com

Lightning Source UK Ltd.
Milton Keynes UK
UKOW031450220911

179110UK00009B/58/P